In Defense of the Marital Family

Law and Religion

Volumes published in this Brill Research Perspectives title are listed at *brill.com/rplrs*

In Defense of the Marital Family

By

John Witte, Jr.

BRILL | NIJHOFF

LEIDEN | BOSTON

Adapted and expanded from *Church, State, and Family* by John Witte, Jr. (Cambridge University Press, 2019). Reproduced with permission of the Licensor through PLSclear.

Library of Congress Control Number: 2023903591

Typeface for the Latin, Greek, and Cyrillic scripts: "Brill". See and download: brill.com/brill-typeface.

ISSN 2468-2985
ISBN 978-90-04-52861-1 (paperback)
ISBN 978-90-04-52860-4 (e-book)

This book is printed on acid-free paper and produced in a sustainable manner.

For Rebecca S. Chopp and Fred Thibodeau

Contents

Preface and Acknowledgments

In 2019, I published a book titled *Church, State, and Family: Reconciling Traditional Teachings and Modern Liberties*, which defended, among other things, the foundational place of the marital family in modern liberal societies. While applauding modern sexual liberties, it also defended the traditional Western teaching that the marital family is an essential cradle of conscience, chrysalis of care, and cornerstone of ordered liberty. It thus urged churches, states, and other social institutions to protect and promote the marital family. It encouraged reticent churches to embrace the rights of women and children, as Christians have long taught. It encouraged modern states to promote responsible sexual freedom and family relations, as liberals have long said. It counseled modern churches and states to share in family law governance, and to resist recent efforts to privatize, abolish, or radically pluralize the marital family. And the book invited fellow citizens and communicants to end their bitter battles over same-sex marriage and tend to the vast family field that urgently needs concerted attention and action.

This much smaller volume is adapted in part from the central chapter of *Church, State, and Family*. It seeks to distill the main traditional Western teachings about the marital family and sketch out their ongoing value and valence, even for late modern liberal societies. It presents the marital family as a sphere, or a globe, with natural and spiritual poles, and with social, economic, communicative, and contractual dimensions radiating between these two poles. This multidimensional marital family unit, I submit, remains foundational for organizing the domestic lives of late modern societies, even those that have adopted more pluralistic marital forms, including same-sex marriage.

Social and political theorists talk a lot about "spheres"—spheres of justice, liberty, love, governance, morality, education, economics, and others.[1] At minimum, these spheres are presented heuristically as descriptions of the distinct institutions or sectors of modern differentiated societies and their respective contributions to private and public life. But talk of spheres is also prescriptive for many theorists today who aim to define and defend more clearly the natural or voluntary associations that buffer the individual from the state. Given

---

1 See, for example, Michael Walzer, *Spheres of Justice: A Defense of Pluralism and Equality* (New York: Basic Books, 2010); Michael G. Kammen, *Spheres of Liberty*, repr. ed. (Jackson: University of Mississippi Press, 2011 [1985]); Stephen B. Post, *Spheres of Love: Toward a New Ethics of the Family* (Dallas, TX: Southern Methodist University Press, 1994); and Harvey Lazar and Christian Leuprecht, eds., *Spheres of Governance* (Montreal/Kingston: McGill-Queens University Press, 2007).

the long and cruel experiences with political tyranny and totalitarianism in the West—even, alas, in our day—many writers have pressed for the separation, independence, freedom, autonomy, or even sovereignty of the spheres of family, church, academy, charity, media, market, and other institutions, both from each other and from the state. Various theories of social or structural pluralism, civil society, voluntary associations, the independent sector, multiculturalism, multinormativity, and other such labels are now crowding the bookshelves—both liberal and conservative, religious and secular, and featuring all manner of methods and logics.

In this volume, I use the metaphor of the marital family sphere both descriptively and prescriptively. I describe the multidimensional marital family sphere as it was historically constructed in the Western tradition and can be reconstructed for modern societies. But in describing the structural complexity of the marital family sphere, I am also resisting efforts by some writers to reduce or flatten the marital family sphere to a single dimension—a mere contract, say, or a simple economic exchange—for these reductionist efforts undercut and undervalue this vital social institution and the public and private goods it offers to late modern liberal societies and their members.

I am grateful to the board and syndics at Cambridge University Press for providing copyright release to repurpose and revise some of the material from *Church, State, and Family* for the present volume. I am also grateful to Lauren Danahy, acquisitions editor for Brill/Nijhoff, and her colleagues for taking on this volume as part of the newly revived book series, Brill Research Perspectives on Law and Religion. It is a special privilege to serve as coeditor of this series with its founding editor, Norman Doe, one of the world's leading scholars of law and religion and director of the Law and Religion Centre at Cardiff University, in Wales. Norman has been a stalwart friend and colleague in the global field of law and religion for many years now, and I am privileged to open yet another new chapter of collaborative work with him.

My thanks to my colleagues in our Emory Center for the Study of Law and Religion who have been stalwart supporters of this work and the bigger volume from which it was adapted. In particular, our Center's senior editor, Dr. Gary S. Hauk, lent his formidable skills to polishing the final manuscript, and the chief of staff, Amy Wheeler, has provided essential administrative services in support of this and other work. My thanks as well to the board and officers of the Lilly Endowment, Inc., as well as of the McDonald Agape Foundation who have generously supported my work in the field of law, religion, and family over the years, including the *Church, State, and Family* book and several earlier titles: *From Sacrament to Contract: Marriage, Religion, and Law in the Western*

Tradition; Sex, Marriage and Family in John Calvin's Geneva; To Have and to Hold: Marrying and its Documentation in Western Christendom, 400–1600; The Sins of the Fathers: The Law and Theology of Illegitimacy Reconsidered; Covenant Marriage in Comparative Perspective; Family Transformed: Religion, Values, and Family Life in Interdisciplinary Perspective; The Western Case for Monogamy over Polygamy; and *Sex, Marriage, and Family in the World Religions.*

I dedicate this publication to cherished friends Rebecca S. Chopp and Fred Thibodeau, who have been such a vital part of my life and the life of my wife, Eliza Ellison, over so many years, and who have been exemplars of the model marital family that I defend in this volume. Rebecca and Eliza were fast friends before Fred and I were on the scene, when they worked together at the Candler School of Theology at Emory University. These two powerful women have been wonderful models of friendship and faithfulness, industry and integrity for so many—not least for Fred and me, who have developed our own special bond of fraternity and friendship over many years. The four of us have enjoyed many meals, hikes, trips, and academic events together while watching our children grow up and eventually form their own marital families.

Rebecca has also been a wonderful supporter of my academic work over the past three decades and more. As provost at Emory University, she greatly enhanced the structure and finances of our law and religion center. Later, as dean of Yale Divinity School, she kindly invited me to give a series of lectures, and repeated those invitations when she was president, successively, of Colgate University and Swarthmore College. Most important, she has been a learned conversation partner about "the weightier matters of the law" and life. I have cherished our long walks together—even when we got hopelessly lost sometimes because the conversation was so engaging.

And so, with Eliza's blessing and applause, I dedicate this volume to Rebecca and Fred, with boundless admiration, appreciation, and affection.

In Defense of the Marital Family

John Witte, Jr.
Center for the Study of Law and Religion, Emory University,
Atlanta, Georgia, USA
john.witte@emory.edu

Abstract

This work combines Christian theology, Enlightenment liberal philosophy, and modern social science to defend the marital family as an essential institution for adults and children, straights and gays alike. John Witte presents the marital family as an integrated sphere with natural, social, economic, communicative, contractual, and spiritual dimensions. He rejects modern efforts to abolish the legal category of marriage or to reduce it to a transient and malleable sexual contract. While celebrating the sexual liberty of consensual adults, Witte calls for stable marital families and responsible sex and parentage as the surest and safest path to private flourishing and social stability for all.

Keywords

marriage – family – children – nature and natural law – social theory – economics of the family – communication – marriage contracts – sacrament of marriage – covenant of marriage – Christianity – Enlightenment liberalism – same sex marriage

Introduction

For better or worse, we are in the midst of a revolution in family law that is upending millennium-long laws and customs of the West. A century ago, a typical Western state defined marriage as an exclusive and enduring monogamous union between a man and a woman with the freedom and capacity to marry each other. Marriage was considered to be the heart of the family and household, designed for the mutual love and support of husband and wife, their mutual protection from sexual temptation, and their mutual procreation, nurture, and education of children. The law required that engagements be formal, and that marriages be contracted with parental consent and witnesses and

 | DOI:10.1163/9789004528604_002

with a suitable waiting period. It required marriage licenses and registration and solemnization before civil or religious authorities. It prohibited marriage and cohabitation by couples with various blood and kin ties or with marital contracts to others. It discouraged marriage where one party was impotent or had a disease that precluded sex and procreation or physically endangered the other spouse. Couples who sought to divorce had to publicize their intentions, petition a court, show adequate cause or fault, and make property provision for the dependent spouse and children after divorce. Criminal laws prohibited fornication, adultery, prostitution, sodomy, polygamy, incest, contraception, abortion, and other sexual offenses. Tort laws held third parties liable for seduction, enticement, loss of consortium, or alienation of the affections of one's spouse. Many of these rules had deep roots in the Western legal tradition, with several rules going deeper still into ancient Greek, Roman, and Mosaic laws.

Today, much of this traditional family law has fallen or been pushed aside in favor of new cultural and constitutional norms of sexual liberty, privacy, and autonomy. Courtship, cohabitation, engagement, marriage, and divorce are now mostly private sexual arrangements with fewer and smaller roles for church and state to play, and fewer restrictions on freedoms of entrance, exercise, and exit. Many states now offer several off-the-rack models of straight and same-sex marriage, civil union, and domestic partnership, with shrinking formal and functional distinctions between them. Privacy laws protect all manner of other voluntary sexual conduct and relationships among consenting adults, and rapidly growing portions of the population—especially those with fewer means and less education—are "drifting into sex and parenthood without marriage."[1] Free-speech laws protect all kinds of sexual expression short of obscenity, but the wildest unregulated frontiers of sexual adventure are now only a mouse click away. Most traditional sex crimes have fallen aside in the West, save rape, sexual assault, and sexual abuse of children, which are now aggressively prosecuted. The classic crimes of incest, prostitution, and polygamy remain on most books, but they are now subjects of emerging academic and constitutional battles. The formal legal categories of marriage and the marital family also remain in place, but leading scholars are now pressing for their expansion, disestablishment, or outright abolition.

---

1 Isabel V. Sawhill, *Generation Unbound: Drifting into Sex and Parenthood Without Marriage* (Washington, DC: Brookings Institution Press, 2014). See further June Carbone and Naomi R. Cahn, *Marriage Markets: How Inequality Is Remaking the American Family* (Oxford: Oxford University Press, 2014).

These exponential changes in modern Western family laws have been, in no small part, valiant efforts to bring greater freedom, choice, and equality to public and private life. They are also basic legal adaptations to the exponential changes that have occurred in the culture and condition of modern families: the stunning advances in reproductive technology; the exposure to vastly different perceptions of sexuality, kinship, and family structure born of globalization; the relaxation and diversification of norms and habits of sexual expression and interaction now greatly enhanced by the internet and other media; and the implosion of the Ozzie and Harriet family as a result of new economic and professional demands on wives, husbands, and children. The sharp reduction of sex crimes further reflects the shift from the traditional "fault-based" system of criminal law that included consensual and victimless sex crimes to a "harm-based" system that focuses on protecting victims from "unwanted sex."[2] The changes afoot reflect shifts from traditional laws heavy on "thou shalt" and "thou shalt not" commands to modern laws focused on nudging and channeling citizens toward more socially desirable sexual behavior. And they reflect a new reliance on the modern welfare state to provide a good deal of the care for "the poor, orphans, widows," and other needy citizens that was traditionally provided by the marital family and broader kin and social networks.

But all these rapid changes have introduced several "striking new separations in the sexual field," in Don Browning's apt words.[3] These separations include those (1) between marriage and sex; (2) between marriage and childbirth; (3) between marriage and childrearing; (4) between childbirth and parenting; (5) between sex and physical contact, given the advent of cybersex; and (6) between childbirth, sexual intercourse, and biological filiation, given the rise of artificial reproductive technology, sperm banks, and surrogacy. Historically, Western churches, states, and societies promoted the integration of marriage, sexual intercourse, childbirth, and childrearing within a sturdy family framework anchored by a stable marriage. Not so much now. As the late Chief Rabbi Jonathan Sacks of the United Kingdom put it:

2 Steven J. Schulhofer, *Unwanted Sex: The Culture of Intimidation and the Failure of Law* (Cambridge, MA: Harvard University Press, 2000).

3 Don S. Browning, "Family Law and Christian Jurisprudence," in *Christianity and Law: An Introduction*, ed. John Witte, Jr. and Frank S. Alexander (Cambridge: Cambridge University Press, 2008), 163–85, at 165–68.

> Sex has become, for the first time since the conversion to Christianity of the Roman Emperor Constantine, an almost value-free zone. Whatever happens between two consenting adults in private is, most people now believe, entirely a matter for them. The law may not intervene; neither may social sanction. It is simply not other people's business. Together with a whole series of other changes, the result has been that what marriage brought together has now split apart. There has been a divorce between sex and love, love and marriage, marriage and reproduction, reproduction and education and nurture. Sex is for pleasure. Love is a feeling, not a commitment. Marriage is now deeply unfashionable. Nurture has been outsourced to specialized child carers. Education is the responsibility of the state. And the consequences of failure are delegated to social workers.[4]

It is easy to lament the breakdown of the modern family and the seeming slide into a sexual state of nature where life is "nasty, brutish, and short," in Thomas Hobbes's words—particularly for women, children, the elderly, and the disabled bereft of reliable kin altruism, diaconal care, or social welfare. Happily, however, in recent years a number of leading scholars, advocates, and religious, cultural, political, and public-health leaders have responded decisively to these exponential changes and are leading a powerful new "modern marriage movement." This movement combines traditional teachings and modern social science and public-health findings to advocate for stable marital families, responsible sex and parentage, and proper family planning as essential for private flourishing and social stability. This movement has pressed for robust new church, state, and economic policies in support of the stable marital family—including, notably, same-sex families.

I have been privileged to be part of this modern pro-family movement, and have worked to help retrieve, reconstruct, and reconcile traditional teachings on the marital family with modern liberties. This volume offers a picture of what the Western tradition has to offer about the public and private goods of the marital family, and how those traditional offerings can be usefully engaged in our late modern societies dedicated to sexual liberty, personal privacy, and domestic autonomy. Part 1 distills some of the basic traditional teaching about the law and theory of the marital family and offers different heuristic models about the structure of the marital family, settling ultimately on the model of the marital family sphere. Parts 2–7 describe each of the six dimensions of this

4 Jonathan Sacks, *The Home We Build Together: Recreating Society* (London: Continuum, 2007), 210.

sphere in turn. The concluding reflections show how an integrated theory of the marital family helps to address a few controversial modern questions of family law, including the heated recent debates about same-sex marriage.

1 The Marital Sphere

Discussions of sex, marriage, and family life have been a vital part of the Western tradition from the very beginning—as they have been in many other traditions.[5] The Bible and various other ancient Near Eastern, Greek, and Roman sources, some going back three thousand years, have offered reflections on the marital household and devised rules and procedures for its proper formation, maintenance, support, dissolution, and succession. While these sources have offered a wide range of teachings about the marital family over the centuries, they also converged on several key features and insights.

Most of these writers supported the same basic legal framework of the Western marital family—much of it constructed before Christianity was on the scene or had much legal influence. In this framework, the marital family was formed by a two-step process—first engagement, then marriage, with a long enough interval between these steps to allow the couple and their families to prepare for the union, exchange property, and invite the material and moral support from the community. Valid engagement and marriage contracts required the mutual consent of a man and a woman who had the age, fitness, and capacity to marry each other. Both contracts could be annulled on discovery of serious impediments like coercion, trickery, mistake, incest, incapacity, or previous marital contracts. Public weddings and feasts were customary final steps in forming a new marriage, although they were not mandatory in the West before the sixteenth century nor feasible for some parties in later eras. Marriage triggered mutual obligations of care and support for the spouses, their children, and their dependents, with reciprocal rights for spouses, parents, and children that could be vindicated by appropriate authorities. Marriage often involved complex exchanges of betrothal gifts and dowry and entailed presumptive rights of dower and inheritance for a widowed spouse and dependent children. Parents and guardians were responsible for the nurture, care, and education of their children and had to prepare them for their own marriages and vocations as adults. Minor children from prior marriages usually joined the new household of their father or mother and became the responsibility

5 For other traditions, see Don S. Browning, M. Christian Green, and John Witte, Jr., eds., *Sex, Marriage and Family in the World Religions* (New York: Columbia University Press, 2006).

of the new couple and family. Adoption was a legal option under civil law and canon law, but not under common law until the turn of the twentieth century. Families were often expected to care for and control servants, students, and apprentices under their roof, and sometimes also provided homes for elderly parents, siblings, and other relatives in a broader marital household. In the first millennium, either spouse could sue for divorce on proof of hard fault, with the subsequent right to remarry. Since medieval times, Catholics have allowed for separation only, not divorce, and permitted remarriage, albeit reluctantly, only after the death of the former spouse or annulment of the prior marriage. Protestants returned to first-millennium rules and allowed fault-based divorce and encouraged remarriage for both parties after a waiting period.

Most of these traditional writers further emphasized the private and public goods of the stable marital family. Classical writers, starting with Aristotle, taught that marriage is a moral, pleasant, and useful institution that provides an efficient pooling of property and division of household labor between husband and wife, a valuable network of kin relatives to enhance one's life, and ideally the blessing of children. The Catholic tradition, starting with Augustine, argued that the marital family has three intrinsic goods: (1) faithfulness and friendship between husband and wife; (2) children, whether natural born or adopted, who carry on the family's name, business, property, and traditions and serve as the next generation of communicants and citizens of church and state; and (3) sacramental stability, an enduring spiritual and temporal institution that gives earthly expression to Christ's sacrificial love for the church and opens an indissoluble channel of God's grace to sanctify the couple, their children, and the broader community. The Protestant tradition, starting with Martin Luther, emphasized further the instrumental goals of the marital family: (1) the mutual protection of men and women from sexual sin and temptation; (2) the love, care, and support of the couple for each other and their kin; and (3) the procreation, nurture, and education of children, who in turn care for their parents as they age and decline.

Early modern household manualists, both Protestant and Catholic, treated the marital family as the first school of love and justice, mercy and discipline, nurture and welfare. Cultivating virtues and vocational discernment in its members, the family provided a model of authority and liberty, charity and sacrifice, industry and discipline for the broader community. Enlightenment philosophers called the marital family the first contract formed as men and women emerged from the state of nature, and the first pillar of an organized society and economy dedicated to the rule of law and the protection of natural rights and liberties of men, women, and children. While the marital family is neither good for everyone nor always good, the tradition has long taught, it offers essential private goods to most couples and children and vital public goods to church, state, economy, and society.

Finally, most of these writers described the marital family as a multidimensional institution. In earlier work, I depicted this traditional teaching with the model of a four-cornered canopy that covers different dimensions of the marital family and its interactions with church, state, society, and nature.[6] In this canopy model, the marital family is a *contractual association*, formed by the mutual consent of the marital couple and their families and subject to their private wills and preferences. It is a *spiritual association*, subject to the creed, code, canons, and ceremonies of the religious community. It is a *social estate*, subject to special state laws of property, inheritance, and evidence and to the expectations and exactions of the public community. And the marital family is a *natural institution*, subject to the natural laws taught by reason and conscience, nature and custom.

These four perspectives, these four corners of the canopy, emphasize different essential features of the institution of marriage—its voluntary formation, religious sanction, social legitimation, and natural origin, respectively. These four perspectives are also linked to competing claims of authority over the marital family—claims by the couple, the church, the state, and nature. When these respective claims and authorities are balanced—when each corner of the canopy is pulled with comparable weight—the marital family is stable. But too much pull in one direction can create imbalance and can even collapse the institution. In earlier work, I used this metaphor to map the main eras of family life and law over the past millennium. In the Middle Ages, the spiritual dimensions of family life under church authority were most prominent. In the early modern era, the social dimensions of the family under state control became more prominent. In the modern era, the contractual dimensions of the household under private control gained ascendency. Now, postmodern culture is privileging self-guided natural views of sexual expression and association, increasingly free from institutional constraints, traditional expectations, or customary practices.

While the canopy metaphor helps describe the evolving historical structure of the marital family, the day-to-day functionality of family life is perhaps better seen in the metaphor of a violin, whose four strings, separately and together, produce the hoped-for harmony of family life. Occasionally one string—the natural, social, contractual, or spiritual—dominates a family's life, but over time all strings get their turn, separately and together, in leading

6 John Witte, Jr., *From Sacrament to Contract: Marriage, Religion, and Law in the Western Tradition*, 2nd ed. (Louisville, KY: Westminster John Knox Press, 2012 [1997]), 1–22.

family life. And they are played at a high or low pitch, a fast or slow tempo, depending on the time and circumstances. Natural feelings and inclinations produce powerful impulses in the first flush of attraction in a courting couple, in the ongoing sexual attraction and intimacy between them, in the immediate deep bonds that form between a parent and child, in the immense mutual sacrifices that husbands and wives, parents and children make instinctually for each other. Contracts are low-key but important moments of negotiation and planning about marital obligations, marital property, parental rights and roles, child support, education, inheritance, and more, and they provide guidance, reliance, and expectation interests for the couple, their children, and the communities around them as the life of the family unfolds. Social interactions and public expectations become important as public betrothals are announced, public weddings are celebrated, new households are registered, new births are celebrated, and the new needs of the family draw in the services of other institutions and professions. And marital families have many spiritual moments and movements, from grand religious weddings to daily family prayers and rituals, from one-time baptisms and other initiation ceremonies to regular catechesis and spiritual formation, from special spiritual ceremonies around birth, marriage, and death to regular family interactions with communities of worship, diaconal care, and education.

While both these metaphors capture different accents and aspects of the marital family, here I offer a bit fuller and more nuanced model of the marital family as a sphere, or a globe—with a natural pole on the bottom, a spiritual pole on top, and various social, economic, communicative, and contractual dimensions radiating between them. At the bottom of this sphere is (1) a *natural* pole that anchors the natural goods of marriage and the inherent human inclinations, appetites, capacities, and imperatives for sex, marriage, and family life. Radiating up from this natural pole are: (2) a *social* dimension that articulates the public communal functions and goods of marriage and the family, and that recognizes the complex groups of institutions and professions that support and interact with the domestic household and its members, not least the church and state; (3) an *economic* dimension that reflects the union of properties, labor, and entitlements by marriage, the ongoing material rights and duties of spouses, parents, and children during and after a marriage, and the channeling, expressive, and signaling functions of modern family law; (4) a *communicative* dimension, expressed in the public liturgies, celebrations, and symbols that mark the formation of a marriage and the birth or confirmation of a child as well as in the vital private daily communications among spouses, children, and household dependents concerning sex, finance, labor, nurture, formation, social responsibilities, and more; and (5) a *contractual* dimension, expressed in the complex formal promises and provisions that form a marriage and household, and the ongoing obligations that attach to the relationships of husband and wife, parent and child, family and society. At the top of the sphere is (6) a *spiritual* pole that helps bind together the natural, social, economic, communicative, and contractual dimensions of the marital family around sacramental, covenantal, or other transcendent ideals, and stipulates the spiritual inspirations and aspirations that marriage and family life provide for husbands and wives, parents and children, and broader communities.

The next Parts take up these six dimensions of the marital family in turn.

2 The Nature of the Marital Family

The Western tradition has long treated the marital family as a "natural" association. The ancient Greeks taught that "Marriage was created by Nature immediately after the dispersal of Chaos," as one Greek liturgist put it. "The ordering of the universe took place because of Marriage and perhaps … Love too was created then." Marriage helped "to create man, and contrived to make him virtually immortal, furnishing successive generations to accompany the passage of time."[7] Moreover, the ancient Greeks thought, marriage helped to complete a person's life. "Love is born into every human being," Plato wrote famously; "it calls back the halves of our original nature together; it tries to make one out of two and heal the wound of human nature."[8] In his *Laws*, Plato thus advised young men to marry "for the city's good" and to restrict "procreative intercourse to its natural function," for such "moderation" will bring "untold good. It is dictated, to begin with, by nature's own voice … and wins men to affection of their wedded wives. There are also numerous other blessings which will follow."[9]

The Bible taught that God created humans as "male and female," called them to join together as "two in one flesh," and commanded them to "be fruitful and multiply" and to fill the earth.[10] God created and inclined the first man and woman to find completion in each other: "This at last is bone of my bones, and flesh of my flesh," Adam said on first meeting Eve.[11] God endowed

7 *Menander Rhetor*, trans. and ed. D. A. Russell and N. G. Wilson (Oxford: Oxford University Press, 1981), 136–39.

8 Plato, *Symposium*, trans. Alexander Nehamas and Paul Woodruff (Indianapolis: Hackett Publishing Co., 1989), 25–31.

9 Plato, *Laws*, VI.773b; VIII.839a–b, in *Plato: The Complete Works*, trans. and ed. Bernard Jowett (New York: Random House, 1965).

10 Genesis 1:26–28.

11 Genesis 2:23.

humans with the physical capacity to join together and beget children. These natural qualities and duties continued after the fall into sin and the expulsion of humans from Paradise, the Judeo-Christian tradition taught. But marriage also served as a remedy to allay sexual sin. Rather than allow sinful people to burn with lust, God provided the institution of marriage so that couples could direct their natural drives and desires toward the service of each other, their children, their kin, and their broader communities. Scores of variations on these stories about the mythical or natural origins of the marital family have echoed in the history of Western thought.

Many Western liberals have been brought up on a social-contract variation of this same idea. It is "self-evident that all men [and women] are created equal and endowed with certain unalienable rights," the argument goes, using the words of the American Declaration of Independence. But in the "state of nature," according to Thomas Hobbes, human life is "solitary, poor, nasty, brutish, and short," a perennial "war of all against all," making it impossible to enjoy and exercise one's natural rights and liberties.[12] Humans thus choose to form contractual associations that provide the structure, support, protection, and predictability needed to enjoy their natural rights as fully as possible. The first such contract they form on exiting the state of nature is the marital contract between a free and equal man and woman. This contract comes before social, political, ecclesiastical, and other private contracts and provides the most basic protection of the natural rights and liberties of men, women, and children. As the first and most fundamental contract, the marital family demands the support and protection of all other contractual associations, including the church, state, society, and economy.[13]

Not only does the marital family have its origins in nature, but family members get guidance from natural law, the Western tradition has long taught. This natural law is, most basically, "the law that nature has taught all animals," giving them "natural inclinations" to protect, preserve, and perpetuate themselves through natural procreative means.[14] Natural law also consists of the natural instincts or intuitions that are unique to humans, and the common

---

12 Thomas Hobbes, *Leviathan*, ed. Noel Malcolm (Oxford: Oxford University Press, 2011), part 1, chap. 12.

13 See, for example, John Locke, *Two Treatises of Government* (1698), ed. Peter Laslett (Cambridge: Cambridge University Press, 1960), II.2–9. 77–83.

14 *Justinian's Institutes*, trans. Peter Birks and Grant McLeod (Ithaca, NY: Cornell University Press, 1987), 1.1.2; *The Digest of Justinian*, ed. Theodor Mommsen and Paul Krüger, trans. Alan Watson, 4 vols. (Philadelphia: University of Pennsylvania Press, 1985), 1.1.3.

customs and conventions that have emerged among humans over time.[15] These distinctly human qualities of natural law are known, refined, and applied in human societies through the exercise of reason and conscience. As both Thomas Aquinas and Hugo Grotius reminded us, many animals, driven only by their natural instincts for self-preservation, kill and eat each other and take each other's homes, food, mates, and offspring. Rational humans, by contrast, have declared these to be crimes of homicide, theft, adultery, and infanticide and have set up laws to deter and punish such harms. Many male animals engage in violent sex, keep harems, and often abandon their mates and offspring. Rational humans, however, have learned to prohibit and punish these acts as crimes of rape, polygamy, and desertion, which defy the natural justice owed to the victim and the community.[16]

Furthermore, humans have learned that exclusive and enduring pair-bonding strategies of marital procreation are the best way to ensure paternal certainty and joint parental investment in their children. This stability is crucial since human babies, unlike the young of most other animals, are born tiny, vulnerable, and utterly dependent on their parents' care for a very long time. Moreover, stable marriages are the best way to ensure that men and women are treated with equal dignity and respect, and that husbands and wives, parents and children, provide each other with support, protection, and edification throughout their lifetimes. The natural law thus inclines humans toward stable marital families. It also encourages humans to outlaw polygamy, fornication, adultery, and easy divorce that violate a spouse's natural rights as well and to outlaw desertion, abuse, neglect, and disinheritance that violate a child's natural rights. Medieval Catholic, early modern Protestant, and liberal Enlightenment thinkers alike have offered numerous variations on this account of the natural foundations of the marital family.

These traditional arguments about the "nature" of the marital family are echoed and elaborated in many quarters today. The recent *Compendium of the Social Doctrine of the Catholic Church*, for example, describes the marital family as the "first natural society" and the "vital cell of society." The family creates a "climate of natural affection" and is a "fundamental structure for 'human ecology.'" It is "the natural community in which human social nature is experienced," and it "makes a unique and irreplaceable contribution to the good of

15 *Decretum Magistri Gratiani*, ed. Emil Friedberg; repr. ed. (Graz: Akademische Druck- u. Verlagsanstalt, 1959), Dist. 1, c. 7.

16 See sources and discussion in John Witte, Jr., *Church, State, and Family: Reconciling Traditional Teachings and Modern Liberties* (Cambridge: Cambridge University Press, 2019), 49–60, 131–40.

society." Indeed, the *Compendium* maintains, "A society built on a family scale is the best guarantee against drifting off course into individualism or collectivism, because within the family the person is always at the centre of attention as an end and never as a means." The *Compendium* affirms "the priority of the family over society and over the State," as the marital family "does not exist for society or the State, but society and the State exist for the family."[17] Hundreds of similar official statements about the nature of the marital family and its foundational place in an orderly society echo through the canons, catechisms, and confessional texts of the modern Catholic Church.[18] Alongside these official church pronouncements, many prominent Catholic scholars at work today in different schools of thought and using different methodologies—including John Finnis, Robert George, Mary Ann Glendon, Stephen Pope, Lisa Cahill, and Russell Hittinger—have offered strong natural-law defenses of the marital family for modern churches, states, and societies.[19]

Prominent modern Protestant scholars, too—ranging from Emil Brunner, Ian Ramsey, and James Gustafson in prior generations[20] to Craig Boyd, Jonathan Burnside, and David Van Drunen today—offer distinct and diverse natural-law accounts of the marital family. They often use inventive scriptural reasoning and skillful reconstruction of classic natural-law teachings on the family by earlier Lutherans, Calvinists, and Anglicans.[21]

---

17 Pontifical Council for Justice and Peace, *Compendium of the Social Doctrine of the Catholic Church* (London: Burns and Oates, 2012), chap. 5.212–14.

18 For the teachings of the modern papacy, see chapters by Russell Hittinger, Stephen Pope, and Robert P. George and Gerard V. Bradley in *Christianity and Family Law: An Introduction*, ed. John Witte, Jr. and Gary S. Hauk (Cambridge: Cambridge University Press, 2017), 323–80.

19 See, for example, John Finnis, *Human Rights and Common Good* (Oxford: Oxford University Press, 2011); Robert P. George and Jean Bethke Elshtain, *The Meaning of Marriage* (New York: Scepter Publishers, 2010); Sherif Girgis, Ryan T. Anderson, and Robert P. George, *What Is Marriage? Man and Woman: A Defense* (New York: Encounter Books, 2012); Stephen J. Pope, *Human Evolution and Christian Ethics* (Cambridge: Cambridge University Press, 2011); Christopher Wolfe, ed., *The Family, Civil Society, and the State* (Lanham, MD: Rowman and Littlefield, 1998); Mary Ann Glendon, *Abortion and Divorce in Western Law* (Cambridge, MA: Harvard University Press, 1987); and Russell Hittinger, *The First Grace: Rediscovering the Natural Law in a Post-Christian World* (Wilmington, DE: ISI Press, 2014).

20 See earlier Protestant views analyzed in Don S. Browning, "A Natural Theory of Marriage," *Zygon* 46 (2011): 733–60.

21 See, for example, Craig A. Boyd, *A Shared Morality: A Narrative Defense of Natural Law Ethics* (Grand Rapids, MI: Brazos Press, 2007); Jonathan P. Burnside, *God, Justice, and Society: Aspects of Law and Legality in the Bible* (Oxford: Oxford University Press, 2011); and David Van Drunen, *Divine Covenant and Moral Order: A Biblical Theology of Natural Law* (Grand Rapids, MI: Eerdmans, 2014).

Leading Anglican theologian Oliver O'Donovan, for example, has written profoundly about the nature of human sexuality, marriage, and family life that is reflected in these biblical and traditional teachings:

> In the ordinance of marriage there was given an end for human relationships, a teleological structure which was a fact of creation and therefore not negotiable. The dimorphic organization of human sexuality, the particular attention of two adults of the opposite sex and of different parents, the setting up of a home distinct from a parental home and the uniting of their lives in a shared life (from which Jesus concluded the unnaturalness of divorce): these form a pattern of human fulfillment which serves the wider end of enabling procreation to occur in a context of affection and loyalty. Whatever happens in history, Christians have wished to say, this is what marriage really is. Particular cultures may have distorted it; individuals may fall short of it. It is to their cost in either case; for it reasserts itself as God's creative intention for human relationships on earth; and it will be with us, in one form or another, as our natural good until (but not after) the kingdom of God shall appear.[22]

O'Donovan has calculated—and lamented—the ample moral, social, and personal "costs" of departing from these "natural goods" of marriage and the family. In particular, he has weighed in on some of the red-hot issues that deeply divide churches, states, and societies today—promiscuity, pornography, contraception, abortion, artificial reproduction, no-fault divorce, extramarital sex, nonmarital birth, same-sex unions, transsexuality, and more. On each of these topics, he has guided his readers to a higher hermeneutical plane, inviting them to see the bigger theological and moral stakes at work in the bitter battles that now beset us about these intimate matters. He has also led readers to a deeper theoretical foundation, encouraging them to look more carefully at the created and natural foundations of sex, marriage, and family life on which a constructive political and theological account of the marital family must build.[23]

Jewish scholars, too, such as David Novak, Elliot Dorff, Ze'ev Falk, and Michael Broyde, have offered powerful accounts of the natural foundation of the marital family, rooting their views in Hebrew scripture and rabbinic

22 Oliver O'Donovan, *Resurrection and Moral Order: An Outline for Evangelical Ethics* (Grand Rapids, MI: Eerdmans, 1986), 69; see further ibid., 20–21, 69–72, 210; and Oliver O'Donovan, *Begotten or Made?*, repr. ed. (Oxford: Oxford University Press, 2002 [1984]).

23 See bibliography and analysis in Robert Song and Brent Waters, eds., *The Authority of the Gospel: Explorations in Moral and Political Theology in Honor of Oliver O'Donovan* (Grand Rapids, MI: Eerdmans, 2015).

jurisprudence.[24] The great Jewish philosopher David Novak, for example, has developed a brilliant account of the "Noachide" foundations of many of the natural forms and functions, rights and duties of the enduring marital household. The natural law born of the covenant between God and Noah after the Flood closely associated marriage with procreation and with the continuation of each people and tribe, Novak writes. After God gave the law at Mount Sinai, Jewish law sanctified this generic marriage idea by connecting its procreative interests with the divine commandment to humans at creation to "be fruitful and multiply." In the later Talmud, the rabbis went beyond those creation imperatives by connecting marriage with the concept of covenant as well. Talmudic Jewish marriages required a public promise in the presence of the covenant community, modeled on the public promises of God to the whole Jewish people. Much as John Selden did four centuries ago, Novak invokes Maimonides to claim that Judaism did not "invent the institution of marriage per se." Rather, Judaism made the natural association of the human family a basic institution of its community, elevated it in the cosmic order, and made it public. But Judaism did all of this "without changing marriage's generic character," which is rooted in a natural law shared by all peoples.[25]

Various scientific studies today offer comparable accounts of the natural foundations of the marital family. For example, in a massive study, *Primeval Kinship: How Pair-Bonding Gave Birth to Human Society* (2008), primatologist Bernard Chapais shows that humans are unique in combining biparental reproduction and the mutual recognition of fathers and their offspring. "The evolution of long-term breeding bonds (pair-bonds) in the course of hominid evolution transformed a promiscuously mating group into a group composed of biparental families," he writes. "From that time on, children were able to recognize their fathers, and the fathers their children." Moreover, humans uniquely developed both "incest revulsion" (avoiding sex with a close blood relative) and "reciprocal exogamous coupling" (having sex with those outside

---

24 See, for example David Novak, *Natural Law in Judaism* (Cambridge: Cambridge University Press, 2008); David Novak, *The Jewish Social Contract: An Essay in Political Theology* (Princeton, NJ: Princeton University Press, 2009); David Novak, *Covenantal Rights: A Study in Jewish Political Theory* (Princeton, NJ: Princeton University Press, 2009); Ze'ev W. Falk, *Jewish Matrimonial Law in the Middle Ages* (Oxford: Oxford University Press, 1966); Louis M. Epstein, *Marriage Laws in the Bible and Talmud* (Cambridge, MA: Harvard University Press, 1942); Michael J. Broyde and Michael Ausubel, eds., *Marriage, Sex, and Family in Judaism* (Lanham, MD: Rowman & Littlefield, 2005).

25 Novak, *Covenantal Rights*, 28. See further David Van Drunen, *Political Theology and Natural Law: Justice, Commerce, and Community Under Noah's Rainbow* (Grand Rapids MI: Zondervan Academic, 2020).

one's own circle). These basic reproductive characteristics form the "deep structure" of human societies in the "transition from nature to culture."[26]

Before humans split off from their chimpanzee and bonobo relatives, Chapais shows, they shared with them the natural building block of "uterine kinship recognition," that is, sibling recognition and favoritism of those offspring born of the same mother. Humans later also developed "agnate-defined kinship," where males began exchanging mates with other male-dominated groups, partially to develop peaceful alliances with their competitors. Females moved from their birth residences to join their male consorts and began to form early signs of pair-bonding, with both females and males recognizing and caring for their tiny and vulnerable offspring. Slowly thereafter, humans developed "stable kin groups, enduring breeding bonds between particular males and females, a dual-phase system of residence patterns (premarital and postmarital), incest avoidance among co-residential close kin, kinship bonds that extend beyond the local group, lifetime bonds between brothers and sisters, … recognition of in-laws, and matrimonial exchange (exchange of spouses between groups)." With this development came what anthropologists call "kin altruism," the preferential attraction and treatment for parents, siblings, and other blood relatives.[27]

All these evolutionary developments were ultimately integrated in the early constructions of the human family, Chapais argues. Pair-bonding, biparentality, and long-term co-residency of male and female in support of their dependent offspring were especially important building blocks of rudimentary forms of the stable marital family among humans. Males began caring for their offspring (or at least showing them preferential treatment), partially to consolidate their relationship to the mother and partially because their own developing cognitive capacities led them to discern that the dependent infant was likely their own, looked and smelled like them, and was part of their own substance. Hence the human natural inclination toward stable pair-bonding patterns of reproduction.[28]

Chapais's book is only one of many evolutionary accounts of the natural origins and development of the human marital family. Some critics have questioned some of the evolutionary steps he describes, and even the teleological premises that he draws from anthropologists such as Claude Levi-Strauss and

26 Bernard Chapais, *Primeval Kinship: How Pair-Bonding Gave Birth to Human Society* (Cambridge, MA: Harvard University Press, 2008), 10–11, 194.

27 Ibid., 12, 35–39, 43–47, 158–63, 190–94, 203–04.

28 Ibid., 194–98. See further Joseph Henrich, Robert Boyd, and Peter J. Richerson, "The Puzzle of Monogamous Marriage," *Philosophical Transactions of the Royal Society B* 367 (2012): 657–69.

Robin Fox.[29] Harsher critics have dismissed all such evolutionary accounts of the natural origins of the human family as little more than the "ethnocentric projection" of the cultural forms of the West to the rest, with too little attention to sexual, marital, and family diversity in the evolving human species.[30] I frankly do not know enough to judge which scientific theories of origins best account for the evidence. But it is clear that Chapais's account has ample support among serious scientists today, even if they differ on details.[31] What is interesting for our story is how these modern scientific accounts, for all their diversity, echo and elaborate various prescientific insights about the nature of the marital family that go back to ancient Greek, Roman, and Jewish sources.

While evolutionary scientists are exploring the natural foundations of the marital family, social scientists are exploring the natural goods that the stable marital family still delivers today in modern Western societies. Their central findings are that, on the whole, it is healthier: (1) to be married or remarried than to remain single, widowed, or divorced; (2) to have two biological or adoptive parents raising a child in a stable household rather than one or none; and (3) to have marital cohabitation rather than nonmarital cohabitation for couples and parents who plan to be together for the long term. On average, these recent studies show, married adults are less likely than nonmarried adults to abuse alcohol, drugs, and other addictive substances. Married parties take fewer mortal and moral risks, and even fewer when they have children. They live longer by several years. They are less likely to attempt or commit suicide, and they enjoy more regular, safe, and satisfying sex, amass and transmit greater per capita wealth, receive better personal health care and hygiene, provide and receive more effective co-insurance and sharing of labor, are more

29 For an appreciative review, see Linda Stone, "Kinship Back on Track: Primatology Unravels the Origin and Evolution of Human Kinship," *Evolutionary Psychology* 6, no. 4 (Oct. 1, 2008); and a careful contextual study in Daniel Cere, "Toward an Integrative Account of Parenthood," in *What is Parenthood: Contemporary Debates about the Family*, ed. Linda C. McClain and Daniel Cere (New York: NYU Press, 2013), 19–40. For a critical review see Robert A. Wilson, "The Primal Path to Kinship: A Critical Review of Bernard Chapais, *Primeval Kinship: How Pair-Bonding Gave Birth to Human Society*," *Biology & Philosophy* 25 (2010): 111–23.

30 See David M. Schneider, *A Critique of the Study of Kinship*, repr. ed. (Ann Arbor: University of Michigan Press, 1984), 95–202, esp. 145–61, 197.

31 See, for example, Melvin A. Konner, *The Evolution of Childhood: Relations, Emotions, Mind* (Cambridge, MA: Harvard University Press, 2010); Peter B. Gray and Kermyt G. Anderson, *Fatherhood: Evolution and Human Paternal Behavior* (Cambridge, MA: Harvard University Press, 2010); Frans B. M. de Waal, *A Tree of Origin: What Primate Behavior Can Tell Us about Human Evolution* (Cambridge, MA: Harvard University Press, 2002); and Frans B. M. de Waal, *Our Inner Ape: A Leading Primatologist Explains Why We Are Who We Are* (New York: Riverhead Books, 2006).

efficient in discharging essential domestic tasks, and enjoy greater overall satisfaction with life measured in a variety of ways. Men, on average, enjoy more of these health benefits of marriage than women, but married women do better on these scores than nonmarried women. The presence of children in the household decreases the short-term benefits, especially for mothers, but it increases the long-term benefits of marriage for both spouses. Most children reared in stable two-parent households perform better in their socialization, education, and development than their peers reared in single- or no-parent homes.[32]

These general social-science data on the health benefits of marriage do not pretend to describe all cases. There are plenty of happy singles. Sometimes the widowed or divorced thrive after surviving or escaping miserable marriages. There are plenty of successful single parents. Sometimes their children thrive in the absence of perennial parental abuse or conflict or in a suitable arrangement for joint custody or visitation. There are plenty of committed couples that transfer smoothly from nonmarital to marital cohabitation. Sometimes such experiments convince couples to forgo marriage to spare themselves and their prospective children the painful costs of divorce. But the recent social-science data suggest strongly that these exceptions, though ample and diverse, do not overcome the basic presumptions about the superior utility and healthiness of monogamous marital unions and intact two-parent families. Modern public-policy experts are taking note.[33] The United States Centers for Disease Control and Prevention, for example, now points to stable marital families as an important condition of private and public health.[34]

---

32 Linda J. Waite and Maggie Gallagher, *The Case for Marriage: Why Married People Are Happier, Healthier and Better Off Financially* (New York: Broadway Books, 2001); and summary of more recent literature in John Witte, Jr., Michael Welker, and Stephen Pickard, eds., *The Impact of the Family on Character Formation, Ethical Education, and the Communication of Values in Late Modern Pluralistic Societies* (Leipzig: Evangelische Verlagsanstalt, 2022).

33 See examples in John Wall, Don Browning, William J. Doherty, and Stephen Post, eds., *Marriage, Health and the Professions* (Grand Rapids, MI: Eerdmans, 2002).

34 https://www.cdc.gov/nchs/data/series/sr_23/sr23_028.pdf. See also Federal Interagency Forum on Child and Family Statistics, *America's Children: Key National Indicators of Well-Being* (Washington, DC: U.S. Government Printing Office, 2015). See ongoing public policy studies in National Marriage Project at the University of Virginia http://nationalmarriageproject.org/; the Institute for American Values, http://www.americanvalues.org/; University of Virginia, Institute for Advanced Studies in Culture, "Culture of American Families," www.isac-culture.org; Benheim-Thoman Center for Research on Child Wellbeing, Princeton University, http://crcw.princeton.edu/; Future of Families and Child Wellbeing Study, Princeton, https://fragilefamilies.princeton.edu/.

To be sure, many scholars today dismiss arguments from nature and natural law as old-fashioned, statist, essentialist, artificial, dogmatic, manipulative, or out of touch with evolutionary, epistemological, or political realities. Moreover, the nature of human sexuality and gender are now subjects of intense debate and legal dispute in some Western circles and media, making appeals to human nature doubly suspect for some. While I am sympathetic with some of these criticisms and movements, natural-law theory has been a staple of the Western legal tradition for two and a half millennia, and it remains a strong school of legal thought and a valuable source of legal argument in courts and legislatures.[35] Moreover, the basic facts of human nature and sexual reproduction have not changed much for most people. Most humans are still social creatures who crave stable intimate and faithful relationships over time. Most people still identify as male or female and are attracted to the opposite gender, even if some now have more fluid (self-)understandings of sexuality and gender. Most humans still have perennial sex drives, especially when they are younger and most fertile. Human babies are still born remarkably small and fragile and remain heavily dependent on adults for a very long time. Women still bond with a child more readily than do men—unless a man is certain he is the father. And humans still decline as they age and become dependent anew on others in their twilight years. These natural conditions of human life and sexuality need to be heeded and addressed in any Western system of family law, even while we now recognize, protect, and in some quarters celebrate new expressions of LGBTQ identity, gender fluidity, and sexual freedom. A family law system must address the natural sexual realities of the entire population, even if our media are fixated on the more sexually fluid, adventuresome, and exotic.

Perhaps a future generation of genomics, cloning, robotics, artificial intelligence, and various new reproductive and childrearing technologies will change these natural conditions. Perhaps a culture will emerge that can deal with human sexuality and reproduction more successfully than the disastrous Soviet experiment of abolishing the marital family at the cost of massive hardship to women and children. Perhaps the West can invent forms and norms of nonmarital reproduction, nurture, and education of children that do not descend into the bleak exploitation of women envisioned in Margaret Atwood's *Handmaid's Tale* or the sterile controlled society envisioned in B. F. Skinner's *Walden Two*. For now, however, such speculation remains the stuff of science

35 See, for example, Norman Doe, ed., *Christianity and Natural Law: An Introduction* (Cambridge: Cambridge University Press, 2017); R. H. Helmholz, *Natural Law in Court: A History of Legal Theory in Practice* (Cambridge, MA: Harvard University Press, 2015).

fiction and utopianism, not jurisprudence and public policy. For the foreseeable future, the natural dimensions of sex, marriage, and family life need to be addressed in any modern theory and law of the marital family.

3 It Takes a Society to Raise a Family

Even the most robust natural law theorists have always understood that the natural configuration of the marital family standing alone is unstable. Human nature and customs might incline us to behave in certain ways in organizing our domestic lives, and many people do follow these natural inclinations without much further prompting. But given the Jekylls and Hydes that perilously reside within all of us, natural inclinations and rational calculus by themselves produce too wobbly a normative framework. In reality, a good number of people stray on occasion from sexual conduct that is healthy and expedient for themselves, their families, and their communities. And a few folks stray all the time, harming others and imposing significant costs by their conduct. Aristotle already saw this: "Just as man is the best of the animals when completed, when separated from law and adjudication he is the worst of all"—especially "with regard to sex and food."[36] American founder James Madison saw it too: "If men were angels, no government would be necessary. If angels were to govern men, neither external nor internal controls … would be necessary … but experience has taught mankind the necessity of auxiliary precautions."[37]

These auxiliary precautions include the many social institutions that stabilize and school natural human inclinations and insights about sex and reproduction. This is the flipside to the traditional teaching that the stable family is the foundation of a well-ordered society. A well-ordered society is just as much the foundation of a stable family. Sociologist Robert Bellah reminds us that without strong social and institutional supports, the marital family is "pitifully vulnerable." Just as "it takes a village to raise a child, … it takes a society to raise a family."[38]

---

36 Aristotle, *Politics*, bk. 1, chap. 2 in *The Complete Works of Aristotle*, ed. Richard McKeon (New York: Random House, 1941).

37 Federalist Paper, No. 51, in *The Federalist Papers: Alexander Hamilton, James Madison, and John Jay*, ed. Ian Shapiro (New Haven, CT: Yale University Press, 2009).

38 See discussion in Robert N. Bellah, "Epilogue: It Takes a Society to Raise a Family," in *Family Transformed: Religion, Values, and Society in American Life*, ed. Steven M. Tipton and John Witte, Jr. (Washington, DC: Georgetown University Press, 2005), 286–98. See further Robert M. Franklin, *Crisis in the Village: Restoring Hope in African American Communities* (Minneapolis, MN: Fortress Press, 2007).

Churches and states are two critical social institutions that have long been tasked with raising the family. Churches for nearly two millennia—and states for even longer—have set out ideals, guides, rules, and procedures for sexual etiquette, courtship, and betrothal; for marital formation, maintenance, and dissolution; for conjugal duties, debts, and desires; for parental roles, rights, and responsibilities. Both church and state also kept overlapping rolls of sexual sin and crime and maintained interlocking tribunals to teach and enforce these rules. The church guided the inner life through its canons, confessionals, and courts, while the state guarded the outer life by policing and punishing sex crimes.

With the liberal reforms and gradual pluralization of Western societies over the past two centuries, most of these legal functions have gradually shifted from the church to the state. Today the modern state dominates Western family law. The state sanctions marital formation and dissolution. State laws nudge, facilitate, and reward citizens for creating and maintaining stable marital households. State officials intervene in family disputes and, when necessary, help dissolve marital families, divide marital properties, and reassign parental responsibilities. State officials protect the rights of family members as well as the sexual liberties of the broader citizenry. State laws facilitate transmitting family property to the next generation and provide victims of sexual harm avenues of redress while punishing sexual criminals.

While the modern state now dominates family law, however, modern churches and other religious communities still help govern some aspects of the family lives of their voluntary members, and some communities still have complex faith-based family-law systems that operate alongside the state.[39] For many couples, the church (and comparably the synagogue, mosque, and temple) remains an important site of marital preparation and weddings. The church is the site of baptisms (and comparable initiation rituals in other communities), where parents and godparents, families and congregations together pledge to love and support and nurture the faith and life of the newly baptized. The church is the site of spiritual formation, where youth learn the ways of God and prepare themselves for public confirmation or profession of faith. The church is sometimes the site of primary education, now usually done in coordination with the state and other social institutions. The church is often the site of diaconal welfare and caretaking—providing food, shelter, care, and emergency relief to widows and orphans, the poor and needy, the stranger and sojourner. The church is sometimes the site of mediation, arbitration, and

39 See overview in Norman Doe, *Christian Law: Contemporary Principles* (Cambridge: Cambridge University Press, 2013).

dispute resolution within families.[40] And the church is the usual site of funerals, which are critical moments of intense pastoral care and support as the family mourns its losses, rearranges its responsibilities, and tends to the needs of family members who are left. All these church services remain profoundly important institutional support for the marital family.[41]

Beyond the church and the state, the Western tradition has long supported the marital family with many other associations and professionals. Long fundamental to the proper formation and functioning of marriage and the family have been the three classic professions of law, theology, and medicine. Legal professionals publish the banns and register the marriage certificates and marital properties of the new married couple. They help enforce, amend, and dissolve the contracts of marriage and marital property. They summon the legal resources to support and protect wives and children from neglect and abuse, and arrange for adoptions, guardianship, and other forms of institutional care and protection. They litigate marital and family disputes in state courts and sometimes church tribunals. They help probate the wills and administer the trusts that are vital to the transmission of the family name and property to the next generation.

Religious professionals, both clerical and lay, provide premarital counseling for the courting couple and consecrate their wedding. They baptize, catechize, and confirm children and provide moral discipline for the household. They provide pastoral care and support for the family and orchestrate involvement of the broader religious community in guiding and nurturing the household and its members.

Medical professionals teach new households the basics of nutrition and hygiene, fitness and aging, child care and development. They provide support, nurture, and care to families during pregnancy and childbirth, sickness or bereavement, abuse or divorce. Medical professionals help ease a person's pain and burdens in the final steps of dying, and they certify death, with all the emotional, spiritual, and legal consequences that follow from this final declaration for the surviving family members.

As Western societies have become more differentiated and specialized, other associations and their professionals have become critical for marriage

---

40 See Michael J. Broyde, *Sharia Tribunals, Rabbinical Courts, and Christian Panels: Religious Arbitration in America and the West* (Oxford: Oxford University Press, 2017); and Michael Helfand, "Arbitration's Counter-Narrative: The Religious Arbitration Paradigm," *Yale Law Journal* 124 (2015): 2994–3051.

41 This paragraph draws on the account of Emil Brunner's views in Don S. Browning and John Witte, Jr., "Emil Brunner," in *Christianity and Family Law: An Introduction*, ed. John Witte, Jr. and Gary S. Hauk (Cambridge: Cambridge University Press, 2017), 307–22.

and the family as well. Therapists now assume a good deal of the psychological and practical counseling for courting couples, broken families, and grieving divorced or widowed persons. Accountants and financiers now participate in a good deal of a family's economics—filing taxes, planning school funds, and devising trusts, wills, and estates. Schools and universities now provide a great deal of the formal education and vocational training historically undertaken by households and churches. Clubs and associations—scout troops, athletic teams, and neighborhood groups—now provide children socialization and skill development. Hospitals and clinics, nurseries and hospices now assume a great deal of the family's health care from the beginning of life to the end.

The family is thus a distinct institution in its own right and an institution deeply interwoven with other institutions. Modern schooling, work, leisure, consumption, worship, legal regulation, and public administration all shape and color the ways we court and marry, bear and raise children, make and break family bonds. At the same time, most people see marriage and family life at the heart of what makes life worth living and essential to a society worth living in and working for. Marriage and family life not only realize romance but also inspire hard work and justify key aims of public policy and provision.[42] In this sense, it does take a society, with all of its diverse institutions, to raise a family. And the breakdown of families causes severe private and public harms that rapidly ripple throughout a community.[43]

To be sure, modern "Americans do not really much like the idea of institutions," Robert Bellah has noted. Critics argue that institutions are holdovers from the past, built on "largely unexamined traditions and habits," and resistant to our current needs and desires. "Institutions are oppressive, at the extreme one thinks of prisons and mental asylums, and they limit our free individual choice."[44] Some family-law scholars today thus call for the "deinstitutionalization," "disestablishment," or "abolition" of the marital family. "Marriage is a great institution, if you like living in institutions," Paula Ettelbrick put it memorably.[45]

42 See further the introduction to Tipton and Witte, *Family Transformed*, 1–2.

43 See an interesting defense of family institutionalism in Priscilla Yamin, *American Marriage: A Political Institution* (Philadelphia: University of Pennsylvania Press, 2012) and more broadly of legal institutionalism in Paul Horwitz, *First Amendment Institutions* (Cambridge, MA: Harvard University Press, 2013).

44 Robert N. Bellah, "Marriage in the Matrix of Habit and History," in Tipton and Witte, *Family Transformed*, 21–33, at 21. See further Robert N. Bellah et al., *The Good Society* (New York: Vintage Books, 1991), 287–306.

45 Paula L. Ettelbrick, "Since When Is Marriage a Path to Liberation?," *Outlook: National Gay and Lesbian Quarterly* 6 (Fall, 1989): 9, 14, quoted and discussed in Stephen Macedo, *Just*

Such criticisms are helpful reminders that all social institutions, including the marital family, must remain coherent, contained, and conducive to private and public goods, and always open to reform and improvement. But it is dangerous to abandon or abolish the institution of the marital family and to leave matters of sex, reproduction, and childcare entirely to unfettered and unstructured free choice. After all, it was the very dangers and violence of a sexual state of nature that forced men and women to form organized societies, with their distinct marital, political, religious, and other voluntary institutions. Brilliant thought experiments about deinstitutionalization and disestablishment of the family are easy enough to draw up on the blackboard or on a blank page or screen. But they are much harder to do in real time and cultural space, with the realities of ongoing social life and the momentum of time-tested customs and family practices. As Bellah put it:

> One of the earliest thinkers to express the modern criticism of inherited institutions was René Descartes in the seventeenth century. At the beginning of the Second Part of one of the founding documents of modernity, *The Discourse on Method*, Descartes describes the typical European town of his day. Such a town is simply a hodge-podge, a jumble of buildings from different eras, in different styles, of different forms, and shapes, and the streets on which they are situated are often crooked, narrow and inconvenient. How much better, says Descartes, if we could just tear the whole thing down and start over, putting up orderly buildings on straight streets with proper right angles. In other words, Descartes's idea of an ideal town is not one inherited from the past, but one designed anew from a rational blueprint. For Descartes the town was a metaphor for our inherited institutions and ways of thought, but in the twentieth century the Romanian dictator Ceauşescu actually did pull down much of old Bucharest and erect "orderly" buildings in its place, with a result that was not charming at all.
>
> Then Descartes makes an even more remarkable move. He regrets that during the early years of his life his mind was filled with opinions, stories and baseless information, entirely unexamined by reason, and he wishes that he might have been born at the age of twenty with his mind uncluttered with so much useless material. I do not even want to think of what kind of monster an unsocialized infant of twenty might be!

Married: Same-Sex Couples, Monogamy & the Future of Marriage (Princeton, NJ: Princeton University Press, 2015), 80–85.

Although every imaginable criticism of institutions, including the institutions of marriage and the family, has some basis, without institutions we would not be free, we would be dead. In every aspect of our lives we depend on the relationships that institutions make possible. This is not in the least to say that they are perfect or that they are not in need of continuous reform and improvement; only that doing away with them altogether is a monstrous idea, as attested by the actions of those in the twentieth century who have tried it, such as Ceauşescu and Pol Pot, though I think some of our rational choice theorists are, in their own way, trying to do something quite similar.[46]

4 The Economics of the Family

Some rational-choice theorists today do, indeed, argue for the freedom to choose prostitution, polygamy, incest, open marriage, à la carte family forms, "take-out" sperm banks, free-market artificial reproductive technology, surrogacy, adoption, baby selling, and more.[47] But many modern theorists—including law-and-economics scholars, who are among the leaders of rational-choice methodology today—have stressed the utility and efficiency of stable marital families and family laws for social and economic life. This is traditional Western lore. Already in the early modern era, household manualists like Richard Baxter pointed out the complex links between the marital household (the *oikos*) and economics (*oikonomika*). These manualists regarded the marital household as a vital economic unit in its own right, especially households with attendant shops, services, apprentices, and servants. They also considered the marital household as a vital source of virtue, discipline, skill, and vocational training central to the success of the broader economic system.[48] Later economic theorists, such as Adam Smith and Jeremy Bentham,

46 Bellah, "Marriage in the Matrix," 21–22, quoting René Descartes, *Discours de la Méthode* (Paris: Larousse, 1934 [1637]), 21–23.

47 See, for example, Richard A. Posner, "The Regulation of the Market in Adoptions," *Boston University Law Review* 67 (1987): 59–72; Elisabeth M. Landes and Richard A. Posner, "The Economics of the Baby Shortage," *The Journal of Legal Studies* 7 (1978): 323–48; and Richard A. Posner, *Sex and Reason* (Cambridge, MA: Harvard University Press, 1992). See other perspectives gathered in Esther Redmont, *The Economics of the Family*, 2 vols. (Santa Barbara, CA: ABC-CLIO LLC, 2015); and Michele Bratcher Goodwin, ed., *Baby Markets: Money and the New Politics of Creating Families* (Cambridge: Cambridge University Press, 2010).

48 See sources and discussion in Witte, *Church, State, and Family*, 106–28.

regarded the stable marital family as an essential institution for modern economic flourishing. For them, the historical development of the marital contract proved to be the most effective means to ensure the community of the mutual care and support of husband and wife and their mutual investment in the nurture and education of their children and kin. The marital family further provided essential security and provision for parents and kin when they became injured, sick, older, and more dependent. And the marital family was a vital conduit to transmit property to the next generation.[49]

Indeed, in premodern Western societies, most marriage contracts were primarily marriage settlements that recorded agreements about transfers of marital property. Although these contracts usually noted the marital consent and familial obligations of the parties, they spent much more ink on the property settlement between the couple and their respective families.[50] Both ancient Jewish law and Roman law had far more detailed laws governing family property and inheritance than any other dimensions of the marital family. Building on these precedents, the Western legal tradition developed an intricate body of law governing family property. This law included the customs, rules, and procedures governing the man's betrothal gift to his fiancée and her family. It included laws directing the woman and her family to deliver a dowry to the new household, while retaining rights to a "marital portion" of this dowry as well as a "dower" interest in her husband's estate on his death, divorce, or desertion. Traditional family law also involved complex and evolving rules for the use, encumbrance, and alienation of marital property by husbands, wives, children, guardians, and trustees. It set out the rights and duties of material support that parents owe their children until their emancipation, and the complex system of child support, marital property division, and (by the seventeenth century) alimony in cases of divorce or annulment. And it included the obligations of children to provide nurture, care, and housing to their elderly parents and needy siblings, with the strong presumption that family members inherit the family property on the death of their loved ones. The economic dimension of marital families—as vital sites of production, consumption, education, welfare, charity, service, business, and property creation, accumulation, distribution, and transmission—has long been a critical feature of Western families and family law.

49 See sources and discussion in ibid., 165–81.

50 See, for example, Philip L. Reynolds and John Witte, Jr., eds., *To Have and to Hold: Marrying and Its Documentation in Western Christendom, 400–1600* (Cambridge: Cambridge University Press, 2007).

4.1 *Rational-Choice Economics*

Some of these earlier norms and forms of family economics still figure in the modern economic analysis of family life and law.[51] One of the most famous formulations was by economist and Nobel laureate Gary Becker, in *A Treatise on the Family* (1981).[52] Becker offered a searching analysis of basic economic principles of production, labor, distribution, and decision-making at work in the marital household, viewed as an economic unit holding valuable "human capital." The "rational choices" at work in human families, Becker argued, allow a person to fulfill a rather simple list of basic needs and desires, including "health, prestige, sensual pleasure, benevolence, or envy."[53] The marital relations of husbands and wives efficiently and directly cater to these basic needs and desires, and rational adults thus choose this institution. When the marriage fails to deliver these goods, the parties divorce and remarry if they can. Moreover, Becker argued, a person's care for his or her children and kin ultimately caters to the same basic needs and desires. For these acts are an indirect but valuable way of serving oneself and continuing one's own existence. Humans are by nature "invested" in the well-being of their offspring and blood kin, because these other family members carry their genes and thereby extend their own existence and influence. Rational humans thus choose to make varying degrees of self-sacrifice for their children and kin, especially when those choices are incentivized and reinforced by powerful cultural signals and legal rewards.[54]

This argument for kin altruism is one of the familiar natural foundations and dimensions of the marital family going back to Aristotle and Aquinas and echoed by Enlightenment liberals and common lawyers. But Becker went

---

51 The next five paragraphs are inspired by Don Browning's analysis of the economic dimensions of the family in Don S. Browning et al., *From Culture Wars to Common Ground: Religion and the American Family Debate*, 2nd ed. (Louisville, KY: Westminster John Knox Press, 2000), 247–70; Don S. Browning, *Reviving Christian Humanism: The New Conversation on Spirituality, Theology, and Psychology* (Minneapolis, MN: Fortress Press, 2010), 127–48; Don S. Browning and Gloria G. Rodriguez, *Reweaving the Social Tapestry: Toward a Public Philosophy and Policy for Families* (New York: W. W. Norton, 2002), 109–30; and Don S. Browning, "The Best Love of the Child? An Integrational View," in *The Best Love of the Child: Being Loved and Being Taught to Love as the First Human Rights*, ed. Timothy P. Jackson (Grand Rapids, MI: Eerdmans, 2011), 365–71.

52 Gary S. Becker, *A Treatise on the Family* (Cambridge, MA: Harvard University Press, 1991). See also Gary S. Becker and Kevin M. Murphy, "The Family and the State," *Journal of Law and Economics*, 31, no. 1 (1988): 1–18.

53 Gary S. Becker, *The Economic Approach to Human Behavior* (Chicago: The University of Chicago Press, 1991), 5.

54 Becker, *Treatise on the Family*, 277–306; see also Posner, *Sex and Reason*, 189.

beyond traditional teaching in assigning calculable economic value to these expressions of family love and kin altruism. He argued that various types of human behavior within the family—including the loving and altruistic behavior of husbands and wives, parents and children, siblings and relatives toward each other—could be understood as human capital that was highly valuable not only to family members themselves but to society as a whole. Moreover, humans have discovered over time that the most efficient way to maximize human capital in the marital household was to divide the labor "between married women, who traditionally have devoted most of their time to childbearing and other domestic activities, and married men, who have hunted, soldiered, farmed, and engaged in other 'market' activities." Becker argued, "Women not only have a heavy biological commitment to the production and feeding of children," but they "have been willing to spend much time and energy caring for their children because they want their heavy biological investment in [re]production to be worthwhile." By contrast, "men have been less biologically committed to the care of children, and have spent their time and energy on food, clothing, protection, and other market activities." The remedy for the resulting gender imbalance in household labor, Becker argued, was the eventual creation of the bilateral marital contract. This contract bound the man to his wife and children and gave women more reliable support for their children as well as protection "against abandonment and other adversities," especially during and after pregnancy. Over time, the long-term marital contract yielded maximum efficiency and value for men, women, children, and their communities.[55]

Becker's economic defense of the intact marital family with a division of labor between stay-at-home moms and go-to-work dads clearly went in a very traditional direction. And his analysis of the rational development of the marital contract in human history echoed the earlier insights of Adam Smith and Jeremy Bentham. One of Becker's insights, however, proved critical for modern family-law reform. That was his call for a better economic valuation of domestic labor within the home. Domestic tasks were typically performed by wives and mothers in the mid-twentieth century, when Becker was writing. But these tasks could be shared or done by men, nannies, grandparents, or other relatives or household workers, as has become more normal today in Western liberal societies. Becker's economic analysis helped us see clearly how cleaning the house, preparing meals, running errands, picking up groceries, raising the children, or helping them with their homework and activities are all valuable forms of work and wealth that contribute to the human capital and value of

55 Becker, *Economic Approach*, 205–14, 264–73; and Becker, *Treatise on the Family*, 30–79.

families as well as individual members within it. Traditional "housework" is just as valuable as "going to work," Becker showed. The value of this housework needs to be taken into much better account in evaluating the role and value of the family in society and the economy, and the respective roles of spouses and parents within and beyond the home. And the value of this domestic labor needs to be better calculated and cashed out to the stay-at-home spouse in the event of divorce or death—not out of pity or patronage, but as a proper economic return on the investment of time and energy in labor. These economic insights—together with powerful feminist arguments for married women's property claims—have helped to render more egalitarian the laws of marriage, divorce, family property, and inheritance in Western lands.[56]

4.2 *Institutional Economics*

Notre Dame family-law scholar Margaret Jane Brinig has used "institutional" law-and-economic analysis to describe and defend the place and value of the stable marital family today.[57] Historically, she notes, marriage was viewed as a sacrament or a "solemn covenant" of "unconditional love and permanence," through which the "parties are bound not only to each other but also to some third party, to God or the community or both." In our modern post-Christian world, however, we need a more neutral metaphor to make this same point. Brinig gets her metaphor from economist Ronald Coase, who wrote on the corporation and the firm. A firm is an association organized to perform a specific function, achieve economies of scale, capitalize on special talents of individual participants, and relate to external parties as a collective unit. Marriage, Brinig argues, is like a firm in that it is based on an agreement between the marital couple and the community about the purpose of this social unit, and how it works internally among its members and relates externally to others. In both firms and families, "this agreement does not purport to anticipate all future transactions among the firm members." Rather, it sets out the structure and procedures of the institution and the obligations of members to meet the

56 See sources and discussion in Witte, *Church, State, and Family*, 341–59; and Witte, *From Sacrament to Contract* 287–314.

57 I have adapted these paragraphs on Margaret Brinig's work from the early manuscript that Don Browning and I were coauthoring before his untimely death in 2010. Portions of these paragraphs later were published in Don S. Browning, "Legal Parenthood, Natural and Legal Rights, and the Best Interests of the Child: An Integrative View," in McClain and Cere, *What is Parenthood*, 105–23, at 116–17.

expectation and interests of other members. "In fact, one of the goals of the firm is elimination of explicit interparty contracting and account keeping."[58]

The addition of children to the marital household introduces a particular type of firm called a franchise, Brinig continues. Franchises distribute, through clear, preexisting channels and agreements, the firm's access to highly valued goods, services, knowledge, and procedures. These may take the form of tasty recipes or products, good customer service, excellent employee training, effective public relations, and trusted reputations. Members and consumers of a franchise flourish when the local unit is well run and plays by the firm's rules in delivering the goods and services. They flounder when the firm's rules are flouted. Just contrast a well-run and a shoddy version of your favorite chain store or restaurant. Marriages with children are like franchises, because the arrival of the child automatically imposes a set of responsibilities, social expectations, shared social capital, mutual obligations, and overlapping histories. Families with children thrive when the parents and kin keep the family unit strong and stable and deliver on the goods and services of nurture, protection, and education that a child needs. Families teeter and can fall apart when they do not deliver consistently or effectively.[59]

Unlike business franchises, however, Brinig argues, families with children cannot be completely dissolved, even after divorce. "Divorcing couples never completely revert to a pre-marriage state. Nor do children leaving home entirely free themselves from their parents or siblings."[60] Their natural bonds and some of the responsibilities of family life and relationships "persist to a certain degree in spite of divorce." This insight reconstructs traditional Christian teachings that the bond or sacrament of marriage remains binding until death, no matter what the parties do or say.[61] It also captures classic common-law teachings that certain family rights and duties remain in place across the generations until the death of all family members.[62]

Brinig has backed up this image of marriage and the marital family as firm and franchise with empirical research that shows how the status and stability of parents in legal marriage is a leading positive asset for the well-being of children. Children do best when the "family franchise" plays by the "marital

58 Margaret Brinig, *From Contract to Covenant: Beyond the Law and Economics of the Family* (Cambridge, MA: Harvard University Press, 2000), 5–7.

59 Ibid., 6–9.

60 Ibid., 7–8.

61 See sources and discussion in Witte, *Church, State, and Family*, 60–64, and Witte, *From Sacrament to Contract*, 65–95.

62 See sources and discussion in Witte, *Church, State, and Family*, 256–72, and Witte, *From Sacrament to Contract*, 305–15.

firm's" structural rules. Brinig and coauthor Steven L. Nock concluded this after exhaustively analyzing the University of Michigan Panel Survey of Income Dynamics and its Child Development Supplement, a massive longitudinal database. They used standard social-science measures of a child's well-being as independently affected by family income, family structure, the legal relation of parents, parental warmth, religious observance, and the mother's race and age. According to their analysis, all these factors count in a child's well-being. But the stable legal marriage of the parents of the child and a stable family structure, especially during the child's tender years, count the most for a child's flourishing. Most children do much better on a host of indices when raised by their own two biological or adoptive parents who live together in a properly contracted and stable family home. Yes, household income contributes amply to a child's well-being; deeply impoverished children fare poorly whether raised in homes with one or two parents. But family income is ultimately not so important to a child's emerging well-being as the legal status of married parents and the stability of the family household. Children do best when they can trust that their home and parental bonds are safe, stable, and supportive.[63]

These findings have concrete implications for family law, Brinig argues. State law should encourage and channel parties to the marital franchise, and not give cohabitation the legal recognition or normalization that can undermine the signaling power of the marital institution. The state should also increase and highlight the social and cultural rewards of marriage and the benefits and privileges that married couples and their children uniquely enjoy. And state law should work hard to stabilize and solidify the relationship between children and responsible adults by a more streamlined law of adoption of new children and stepchildren in marital homes.[64] All this, too, is a modern variation on traditional lore. Twenty-five hundred years ago, Aristotle argued that it was "just" for the polis to pass laws encouraging couples to marry and procreate within stable families. Two hundred fifty years ago, William Paley and the utilitarians argued that it was "expedient" for state laws to encourage stable marital families rather than allow "sexual libertinism" to reduce the incentives

63 Margaret F. Brinig and Steven L. Nock, "Legal Status and Effects on Children," *University of St. Thomas Law Journal* 5 (2008): 548–79; Margaret F. Brinig and Steven L. Nock, "Can Law Shape the Development of Unconditional Love in Children?" in Jackson, *The Best Love of the Child*, 317–46, at 330–37; Margaret F. Brinig and Steven L. Nock, "'I Only Want Trust:' Norms and Autonomy," *Journal of Socio-Economics* 32 (2003): 471–87; and Margaret F. Brinig, *Family, Law, and Community: Supporting the Covenant* (Chicago: University of Chicago Press, 2012).

64 Brinig, *From Contract to Covenant*, 28–29, 208–22.

for entering and maintaining a marriage.[65] Today, law-and-economics scholars are making comparable arguments, now backed with empirical data.

4.3 *Behavioral Economics*

Brinig's language of "signaling" and "channeling" points to a third branch of modern economics that has weighed in heavily on the modern family and family law. This is the field of behavioral economics, where Nobel laureate Richard Thaler and other distinguished scholars have made strong contributions.[66] Behavioral economists argue that state laws exercise an important *channeling* function by supporting social institutions or practices that promote health, safety, and welfare. Instead of using "thou shalt" or "thou shalt not" commands, the channeling function of law nudges citizens toward certain behavior and away from others. This happens with individual behaviors in many areas of life. The state often facilitates, licenses, encourages, sometimes even pays for or rewards desirable behavior. Think of voting in a state election, getting a free flu shot or COVID vaccine, or going to college on a state scholarship. As for undesirable behavior, the state will sometimes impose taxes or fines on it or withhold benefits for those who indulge in it. Think of smoking, not wearing seat belts, or dropping out of high school. The theory of legal channeling stipulates that, over time, the more desirable behavior so encouraged by the state will become more customary, even natural or reflexive, and the undesirable behavior will be viewed as aberrant and perhaps even stigmatized.

The channeling function of law also works at the institutional level, writes University of Michigan family-law scholar Carl Schneider.[67] The modern corporation is a good example, he writes. The law channels businesses, merchants, and investors to use this legal form for economic transactions. The state gives the corporation a special set of rights and benefits, including the ability to hold property in perpetuity, to limit personal liability for officers and investors, to

65 See sources and discussion in Witte, *From Sacrament to Contract*, 18–20, and Witte, *Church, State, and Family*, 170–75.

66 See, for example, Richard H. Thaler and Cass R. Sunstein, *Nudge: Improving Decisions about Health, Wealth, and Happiness* (New York: Penguin Books, 2008); Robert Ellickson, *The Household: Informal Order around the Hearth* (Princeton, NJ: Princeton University Press, 2008); Eric A. Posner, *Law and Social Norms* (Cambridge, MA: Harvard University Press, 2000); Eric A. Posner, ed., *Social Norms, Nonlegal Sanctions and the Law* (Northampton, MA: Edward Elgar, 2007); and Richard H. McAdams, *The Expressive Powers of Law: Theories and Limits* (Cambridge, MA: Harvard University Press 2015).

67 Carl E. Schneider, "The Channeling Function in Family Law," *Hofstra Law Review* 20 (1992): 495–532, at 498, 503–04. See further Carl E. Schneider and Margaret F. Brinig, *An Invitation to Family Law: Principles, Process, and Perspectives*, 3rd ed. (St. Paul, MN: West Publishing, 2006), 211–21, 507–09.

reduce taxes, and to survive over time and in different places at once. Because of the law's channeling function, the corporate form "has become familiar, natural, and comfortable" for most citizens, Schneider writes. Enterprises small and large are now attracted to it, and the law facilitates corporate formation, investment, accountability, and dissolution through specialized corporate laws. While businesses can and do use other legal forms, the corporation is now the default legal position in many Western societies.[68]

The marital family is a comparable institution that state law needs to "shape, sponsor, and sustain," Schneider argues, given the public and private goods it offers. The state should continue to recognize and preserve the marital family as a valuable, even superior, form of intimate association, and the state should channel, nudge, signal, and recruit adult parties toward participation in it. Like the corporation, the institution of marriage offers various legal benefits, privileges, and rights not available to other domestic unions. And like corporate law, family law sets easy default rules for parties who wish to enter this institution, rather than forcing parties to create this legal form from scratch or forgo its legal benefits. The modern state cannot require parties to marry or to have or forgo children. Indeed, constitutional law now protects sexual intimacy, cohabitation, contraception, and procreation by natural or artificial means without marriage. But the channeling function of family law, political theorist Stephen Macedo writes in glossing Schneider, helps create and normalize "the social expectation that people ought to get married [as] a kind of rite of maturity" and to raise their children so much as possible in an intact marital family.[69]

Alongside channeling, Schneider continues, family law also has an *expressive* function. It "provides a voice in which citizens may speak," and it can "alter the behavior of people the law addresses."[70] This expressive function has always been important in Western family law. By law, historically, public betrothals were announced by town criers, preachers, or posted banns; while this expressive function now takes the form of voluntary announcements in local newspapers, wedding invitations, marriage registries, and Facebook postings, its importance remains. By law after the sixteenth century, and by custom for many centuries before, weddings were public ceremonies and celebrations—now culminating with the final statement from the presiding official, "by the power of the state vested in me, I pronounce you husband and wife." By law, the newly married couple registered their marriage with the state,

68 Schneider, "The Channeling Function," 499.
69 Ibid., 498; and Macedo, *Just Married*, 92–97.
70 Schneider, "The Channeling Function," 499–501.

expressing to themselves and the world that they now have a new status as a marital couple and marital household. By law, a newly born or adopted child triggered not only private announcements but also a state birth certificate announcing the child's name, place, and time of birth, and the name of the parents, the most responsible parties for that child. All these expressive legal steps are designed to alter the behavior of people, not only the new couple and family but also their neighbors. The community is invited to support the new couple and family, to respect their new marital bond and family privacy, and to hold these parties accountable to the commitments they have made to each other and their children. "Marriage is the 'committed relationship' par excellence," Macedo writes. And by entering into a legal marriage, a couple expresses to the world that they are "making this commitment … to particular principles, people, and projects, and carrying those commitments forward over decades," faithfully, flexibly, and fully for each other and their children.[71]

International family-law scholar Marsha Garrison uses the related concept of "signaling" that a formal state-sanctioned marriage allows a couple to make:

> Formal marriage signals intention. It signals each partner who enters into a new marital union, their friends, and their families. It also signals strangers; those who meet or do business with the married couple understand that each spouse has entered into a binding commitment that entails expectations of fidelity, sharing, and lifetime partnership. Formal marriage also signals intention to the state; government officials can and do assume that the married couple has undertaken obligations to each other.… Formal marriage accomplishes all of these signaling functions prospectively, efficiently, and unequivocally. After a couple marries, there is no question about what sort of relationship they intend. No litigation will be necessary to determine their relational status. No decisionmaker will be required to sift through heaps of self-serving testimony about individual promises made and understandings reached.[72]

These three schools of rational-choice, institutional, and behavioral economic analysis of the family underscore an insight going back to Aristotle: that the marital household (the *oikos*) and the discipline of economics (*oikonomika*) are organically interlinked. The marital household has long been a vital economic

71 Macedo, *Just Married*, 92–93. See also Martha C. Nussbaum, "A Right to Marry?" *California Law Review* 98 (2010): 667–96.

72 Marsha Garrison, "The Decline of Formal Marriage: Inevitable or Reversable?" *Family Law Quarterly* 41 (2007–2008): 491–520, at 493.

unit of its own—especially households with attendant farms, shops, services, and servants which depend on and contribute to stable markets and currencies. It has also long been a vital source of education, apprenticing, and vocational training central to the success of economic, political, and religious life. The household has long provided essential security and provision for parents, children, and other kin, for caring and sharing, nutrition and nursing, welfare and poor relief when household members became impoverished injured, incapacitated, sick, elderly, or otherwise dependent—even if these tasks are now shared more fully with other social institutions and professions and by the modern welfare state in Western lands. And the formation of a new marital family is often a critical time of property and financial exchange between two families in a prior generation, and it provides a fundamental conduit for transmitting property to the next generation through gift, trust, donation, inheritance, and more.

Rational-choice economists have taught us to assign economic values to these vital family services. Institutional economists have provided models and measures for how marital families can maximize their values for spouses and children. And behavioral economists have shown how states, churches, and other institutions can nudge, signal, and channel parties in encouraging them to choose healthy marital family lives.

5 The Communicative Dimensions of the Family

The channeling, expressive, and signaling functions of church, state, and society are part of the complex communicative dimensions of the marital family: complex because so many different sectors of society are in communication about the marital family and its members; complex in that the modes of communication range from subtle signals and nudges to overt statements and visual media depictions; and complex because of the range of subjects being communicated.

The marital family is not only the object of communication by other institutions, however. It is also the site and subject of unique forms of communication between husband and wife, parents and children. This, too, is an ancient and enduring teaching in the West. In the fifth century, the Greek Church Father John Chrysostom called for "constant and open communication" between husband and wife. Sounding much like a modern marriage therapist, he pointed to the "symphony" of verbal, affectionate, sexual, financial, parental, and management communication that becomes a healthy marriage and marital household. He also urged couples to appreciate the more subtle and sensitive symbolic, sacrificial, and symbiotic ways that spouses learn to intuit and respond to each other's needs, cares, and desires. For Chrysostom, marriages are "incarnations" of divine love, sacrifice, and commitment; families are "living icons" of traditions, memories, and rituals.[73] In the seventeenth century, English poet John Milton wrote similarly that "the apt and cheerful conversation of man with woman is the chief and noblest purpose of marriage." "Where loving [conversation] cannot be, there can be left of wedlock nothing but the empty husk of an outside matrimony"—dry, shriveled, and dispensable. Aptness can strain cheerfulness: candid conversations between spouses can be painful. Cheerfulness can strain aptness: blissful domestic ignorance can be tempting. But aptness and cheerfulness properly belong together in a marriage, Milton tells us. Where they fail, the marriage fails.[74]

Today, communication remains "the dynamic side" of community, writes Oliver O'Donovan, "the treating of goods as common and the readiness to discern private interest only insofar as it is compatible with common interest."[75] As social creatures, we inhabit many communities of communication—political communities into which we are born, religious communities into which we are initiated, neighborhood communities in which we live, and sundry other communities that we inhabit or seek out for work, play, education, investment, pleasure, consumption, art, science, health care, services, and more. Each of these communities has its distinct norms and forms of communication that convey meaning, purpose, promise, or friendship.[76]

But the most sublime, intense, and enduring forms of communication usually occur within marriage. In marriage, we are the most intimate: we communicate our deepest feelings, passions, fears, aspirations, intuitions, and experiences with our spouse. In marriage, we are the most vulnerable: we share our very life, body, memories, health, happiness, well-being, food, money, and material goods with our spouse. And in marriage we are the most fully committed: marriage carries an expectation of fidelity, loyalty, and permanence that is communicated in the daily sharing of life, home, bed, and board and goes beyond that of any other community.

Communication is also at the heart of the relationship of parents and children. Berkeley law professor John E. Coons has written memorably about

73 See sources and discussion in Witte, *Church, State, and Family*, 20–29.

74 See sources and discussion in Witte, *From Sacrament to Contract*, 269–86.

75 Oliver O'Donovan, *Entering into Rest: Ethics as Theology*, vol. 3 (Grand Rapids, MI: Eerdmans, 2017), 47–48.

76 Ibid., 63–64, 140–46.

the creative power of words. By words, God created the world. "God *said*, 'let there be,' … and there was." So it is with procreation, Coons writes. "In a faint echo of the divine, children are the most important Word most of us will utter."[77] We communicate our very substance to our children—our genes, we now say, coded and coated with our instincts, inclinations, talents, strengths, weaknesses, resiliencies, and vulnerabilities. Mothers communicate their very bodies, blood, and being with their children throughout pregnancy, and then provide their newborns with life-giving food and drink through nursing. Parents share the tender singing, cooing, rocking, cuddling, and caressing that communicate the deep feelings of love and tenderness so vital to a child's well-being and healthy development. Developmental psychologist Erik Erikson once wrote that the first "greeting ceremonial" between a mother and a child "is the root of all subsequent ritualization" and communication.[78]

Both parents' and the broader family's verbal and symbolic communications prove vital for the child's healthy development and maturation. This communication occurs in morning and bedtime rituals, table talks over meals, the lessons of reading, playing, praying, working, and interacting with parents, siblings, friends, and kinfolk in all kinds of ways.[79] The Western tradition has long understood this. The Bible and other ancient texts called parents to communicate and commend the laws, traditions, and ways of God's people: "You shall teach them diligently to your children, and shall talk of them when you sit in your house and when you walk by the way, and when you lie down and when you rise."[80] "Make them known to your children and children's children."[81] Such passages, and their many parallels in classic literature,[82] have inspired a long and deep tradition of reflection about how critical these evolving forms

77 John E. Coons, "The Religious Rights of Children," in *Religious Human Rights in Global Perspective: Religious Perspectives*, ed. John Witte, Jr. and Johan D. van der Vyver (The Hague: Martinus Nijhoff Publishers, 1996), 157–74, at 172. See further John E. Coons and Patrick M. Brennan, *By Nature Equal: The Anatomy of a Western Insight* (Princeton: Princeton University Press, 1999), 55–59.

78 Erik Erikson, "The Development of Ritualization," in *The Religious Situation*, ed. Donald R. Cutler (Boston: Beacon Press, 1968), 711–33, quoted and discussed in Bellah, "Marriage in the Matrix," 25.

79 See, for example, Robyn Fivush, *Family Narratives and the Development of an Autobiographical Self* (London: Routledge, 2019); and Robyn Fivush and Judith A. Hudson, eds., *Knowing and Remembering in Young Children* (Cambridge: Cambridge University Press, 2013).

80 Deuteronomy 6:6–9.

81 Deuteronomy 4:9.

82 See, for example Judith Evans Grubbs et al., eds., *The Oxford Handbook of Childhood and Education in the Classical World* (Oxford: Oxford University Press, 2014); and Nicholas Orme, *Medieval Children* (New Haven, CT: Yale University Press, 2001).

of communication are for a child's spiritual, moral, emotional, intellectual, and social formation. Books on child education, development, catechesis, and formation have, accordingly, been staples of the Western tradition from the start.[83] The early modern household manualists sought to routinize all this lore in hundreds of pages of rules, illustrations, pictures, and vignettes, helping parents and children understand and work through the escalating complexities of communication at different stages of the family life cycle. These have been replaced by a whole literary and virtual industry of child-rearing guides and therapeutic services today, religious and secular alike.[84]

Many siblings and relatives also share a deep and enduring communicative bond with each other, in part because of their natural ties, in part because of their common experiences. There are many touching stories of mothers and children or twins, separated from each other at birth for various reasons, who have intuitive recognition and instant communication on first seeing each other later in life. Even children born of sperm donation experience some of this sensation on discovery of their biological fathers.[85] Not just natural ties but also common experience and communication are at work as siblings and other relatives slowly spin and stitch together the fabric of symbiotic attachment and communication that can last a lifetime, and that siblings can often pick up easily again, even after long intervals of silence and separation.

Communication with and within the marital family comes not only in daily routines and interactions. Communication at full volume and valence marks the great days of ritual celebration in the life of a marital family. The most prominent such occasions are weddings, which can be extravagant symphonies of communication, featuring rich liturgies and vows, triumphant music and dancing, beautiful clothes, flowers and jewels, food and drink, often shared with extended family and friends. Weddings are ancient ceremonies in the Western tradition and beyond.[86] In the Jewish tradition, the Talmud provided detailed liturgies and prayers for both betrothal and marriage, building in part

---

83 Marcia J. Bunge, ed., *The Child in Christian Thought and Practice* (Grand Rapids, MI: Eerdmans, 2000).

84 See sources and discussion in Witte, *Church, State, and Family*, 106–28.

85 Elizabeth Marquardt, *My Daddy's Name Is Donor: A New Study of Young Adults Conceived through Sperm Donation* (New York: National Marriage Project, 2011); Carolyn Campbell, *Together Again: True Stories of Birth Parents and Adopted Children Reunited* (New York: Berkley Books, 1999); Richard J. Blauwhoff, "Tracing Down the Historical Development of the Legal Concept of the Right to Know One's Origins," in *Debates in Family Law around the Globe at the Dawn of the 21st Century*, ed. Katharina Boele-Woelki (Antwerp: Intersentia, 2009), 145–70.

86 See examples in Don S. Browning, M. Christian Green, and John Witte, Jr., eds., *Sex, Marriage and Family in the World Religions* (New York: Columbia University Press, 2006).

on prototypes in the Book of Tobit. These weddings were essential community events, presided over by the rabbi and involving the entire local community.[87] The Christian tradition celebrated weddings from the start, though the earliest surviving marriage liturgies are from the eighth century.[88] Particularly among the Eastern Orthodox, these liturgies became extraordinary visual and verbal dramas of prayer, blessing, oaths, and rituals, including the Eucharist. Wedding liturgies grew more slowly in the Christian West, not becoming mandatory among Catholics until 1563, and subject to wide and perennial variation among Protestants. Great wedding feasts are often echoed on major wedding anniversaries—silver and gold, in particular—sometimes featuring the renewal of marital vows, with accompanying rings and jewels to underscore this new commitment. Childbirth, baptism, and other initiation rituals are also times for rich ceremonies and celebrations, filled with verbal and symbolic communication for families, friends, and fellow congregants alike to witness and to weigh in with pledges and promises of support and protection of the new child and parents.

6 The Contractual Dimensions of the Marital Family

The private and public communications of promise and commitment in marriage underscore the two final dimensions of the marital family sphere—the contractual and the spiritual. The contractual dimension, featuring the mutual promises and ongoing rights and duties of husbands and wives and of parents and children, has been a perennially prominent emphasis of the Western legal tradition, even if church and state have sometimes vied for control of these contracts. The spiritual dimension of the marital family has changed in definition and importance, especially in recent decades, but most parties still agree that "marriage is more than a mere contract"; it is a bond of "just love" and "abiding friendship" that transcends any other human relationship.[89]

6.1 *Husbands and Wives*

John Calvin reminded us that marriage may be "more than a mere contract, but it is not less than a contract."[90] In the Western legal tradition, a valid marriage

87 Kenneth W. Stevenson, *Nuptial Blessing* (New York: Oxford University Press, 1982), 3–8.

88 Ibid., 33–122, with samples in Mark Searle and Kenneth W. Stevenson, *Documents of the Marriage Liturgy* (Collegeville, MN: Liturgical Press, 1992).

89 Margaret A. Farley, *Just Love: A Framework for Christian Sexual Ethics* (New York: Continuum, 2008).

90 See sources and discussion in Witte, *Church, State, and Family*, 88–105.

depended in its essence on the mutual consent of the man and the woman. Even if the prospective bride and groom were represented by parents or guardians during the contract negotiation, their own consent to the marriage was essential. While Western authorities have tolerated arranged marriages and child marriages, particularly when those were politically or commercially advantageous, in theory both the man and the woman reserved the right to dissent from the arrangement upon reaching the age of consent, leading to annulment of the engagement or marriage. Moreover, Western authorities since biblical and classical times have warned parents and guardians against bullying children into unwanted unions. These protections for children have become stronger since early modern times, as the rights of children were set out more fully.[91]

While persons were free to choose or to forgo marriage, they were not free to marry just anyone, anytime, or on any terms. Both parties had to be of the age of consent, with the mental, physical, and sexual capacity to enter a marital contract with each other. They could not marry anyone related to them by blood or by marriage, or related to another by an existing marital contract; these were the impediments of consanguinity, affinity, and precontract that led to annulment. For many centuries, prospective spouses had to be of comparable social and economic status and age and, ideally (in some traditions, indispensably), of the same faith. The parties had to follow proper contractual forms and ceremonies, and younger parties needed the consent of both sets of parents or guardians, especially for a first-time marriage.

Legal requirements for valid marital formation are more flexible and fluid today. In growing numbers of Western countries, adults may now choose a same-sex spouse and marry someone of quite different socioeconomic status, culture, religion, or age. Parental consent, community participation, and liturgical celebration of marriage are less essential than they were in early modern times. But other conditions to a valid marriage contract, most importantly the demand for full and free consent on both sides, remain firmly in place in Western family law.

Many of the built-in obligations of the marital contract also remain. Ancient Jewish law required husbands to provide their wives with clothing, protection, support, sex, medical help, ransom, dower, and inheritance, on pain of communal censure or threat of divorce.[92] Early Christian canon laws and penitential texts, building on both the Old and New Testaments, set out comparable

91 See sources and discussion in ibid., 81–84, 152–60, 256–72.

92 See sources and discussion in ibid., 140–48; John Witte, Jr., *The Sins of the Fathers: The Law and Theology of Illegitimacy Reconsidered* (Cambridge: Cambridge University Press,

mutual duties of husbands and wives, which were enforceable eventually in church courts. Medieval confessional manuals and early modern household manuals alike detailed the rights and duties that spouses owed each other throughout their lives and the testamentary duties to each other and to their children after death.[93] Still today, lawfully married spouses have automatic contractual duties of mutual support, protection, and care, backed by laws of crime, tort, and divorce. Modern laws still protect basic spousal evidentiary privileges and immunities, joint family property ownership, and rights to make vital health and medical decisions as surrogates for one's spouse and children. American laws still grant a surviving spouse strong claims to the late spouse's estates, insurance proceeds, residual social security and veteran benefits, and other entitlements. To be sure, couples today may create elaborate prenuptial contracts that differ somewhat from the default marital rules held out by the state, so long as the essentials of marriage are not subverted. But for most couples, the state's family law creates convenient frameworks of spousal rights and duties to facilitate their relationship and to identify and clarify the reliance and expectation interests they bring to the relationship.[94]

While these contractual rights and duties were historically rooted in biblical and theological worldviews, and sometimes enforced by religious authorities, the modern Anglo-American common-law tradition settled on the idea that marriage is a status with preset contractual terms enforced by the state alone. Prospective couples were free to accept or reject the marital contract, but they could not alter its essential terms. American family lawyer Joel Bishop put it nearly two centuries ago:

> [Marriage is] a civil status, existing in one man and one woman, legally united for life, for those civil and social purposes which are founded in the distinction of sex. Its source is the law of nature, whence it has flowed into the municipal laws of every civilized country, and into the general law of nations.... [M]arriage may be said to proceed from a civil contract

---

2009), 16–26. See further Leo G. Perdue, ed., *The Family in Ancient Israel* (Louisville, KY: Westminster John Knox Press, 1997); and Epstein, *Marriage Laws in the Bible and Talmud.*

93 Carolyn Osiek and David Balch, *Families in the New Testament World: Households and House Churches* (Louisville, KY: Westminster John Knox Press, 1997); James A. Brundage, *Law, Sex, and Christian Society in Medieval Europe* (Chicago: University of Chicago Press, 1987), 51–175; and Pierre Payer, *Sex and the Penitentials: The Development of a Sexual Code, 500–1550* (Toronto: University of Toronto Press, 1994).

94 See sources and discussions in Linda C. McClain, *The Place of Families: Fostering Capacity, Equality, and Responsibility* (Cambridge: Cambridge University Press, 2006); and Anita Bernstein, "For and Against Marriage: A Revision," *Michigan Law Review* 102 (2003): 129–212.

> between one man and one woman, of the needful physical and civil capacity. While the contract remains executory, that is, an agreement to marry, it differs in no essential particulars from other civil contracts.... But when it becomes executed in what the law recognizes as a valid marriage, its nature as a contract is merged in the higher nature of the status.[95]

"The doctrine that marriage is a *status* is modern," added Bishop's fellow family lawyer William Nelson.[96] It is halfway between the traditional notion that "marriage was a [public] sacrament to be solemnized by a religious ceremony of the church regardless of the faith of the parties" and the notion that marriage is a private "*civil* contract," in whose terms, conditions, and performance the public and state have no interest. Marriage was a contract, but it was also more than a contract, because so many of its terms were preset by nature and society and not negotiable. Marriage was less than a sacrament, but it did embrace some of the same qualities of faithfulness, exclusivity, and presumptive permanence that typified Western sacramental and covenantal marriages since biblical times.[97]

Although many scholars of Western family law are now calling for the liberation of sex and the "private ordering" of domestic affairs without preset contractual rights and duties,[98] others still defend the value and utility of the state maintaining status rules for marriage, even while recognizing greater sexual liberty.[99] Carl Schneider and Margaret Brinig, we have seen, argued that stable and clear marital commitments are critical to the well-being and trust of children and spouses. Marsha Garrison has argued that signaling such

95 Joel Prentiss Bishop, *Commentaries on the Law of Marriage and Divorce, and Evidence in Matrimonial Suits*, 2nd ed. (Boston: Little, Brown, & Co. 1856), 25. See also James Schouler and Arthur W. Blakemore, *A Treatise on the Law of Marriage, Divorce, Separation, and Domestic Relations*, 6th ed. (Albany, NY: M. Bender & Co., 1921), 2:1346.

96 William T. Nelson, *A Treatise on the Law of Divorce and Annulment of Marriage* (Chicago: Callaghan & Co., 1895), 1:5.

97 Ibid., 5–8; see also Joseph R. Long, *A Treatise on the Law of Domestic Relations*, 3rd ed. (Indianapolis: Bobbs-Merrill, 1923), 3–10.

98 See sources and discussion below in Witte, *Church, State, and Family*, 336–41.

99 See, for example, James E. Fleming and Linda C. McClain, *Ordered Liberty: Rights, Responsibilities, and Virtues* (Cambridge, MA: Harvard University Press, 2013); Marsha Garrison and Elizabeth Scott, eds., *Marriage at the Crossroads: Law, Policy, and the Brave New World of Twenty-First Century Families* (Cambridge: Cambridge University Press, 2013); Elizabeth S. Scott, "A World without Marriage," *Family Law Quarterly* 41 (2007): 537–66; Elizabeth S. Scott and Robert E. Scott, "From Contract to Status: Collaboration and the Evolution of Novel Family Relationships," *Columbia Law Review* 115 (2015): 293–374; and Anita Bernstein, ed., *Marriage Proposals: Questioning a Legal Status* (New York: NYU Press, 2006).

clear commitments is critical for society, too, providing "a certain and efficient method of registering relational intentions that cannot be obtained through informal mechanisms."[100] Elizabeth Scott and Robert Scott have called for the creation of "collaborative techniques to build trust and confidence" among various nonmarital cohabitants so they can make a "long term commitment to mutual care and interdependence ... to satisfy members' dependency needs" and move smoothly down "the path from contract to status."[101] Milton Regan has argued that clear default rules about the rights and duties of marital status enhance rather than erode personal freedom. "[T]hose who invoke the value of private ordering to criticize preferential treatment for marriage overlook the fact that in certain respects those who marry have more latitude to arrange their relationships as they wish than those who cohabit."[102] A clearly delineated marital contract creates more certainty of a person's status and obligations in an increasingly mobile, anonymous, and diverse world often devoid of local expectations and accountability and customary constraints. Moreover, "marriage has such cultural resonance because it is seen as involving an open-ended pledge to share the uncertainties of life 'for better or for worse,' rather than a qualified promise to bear some risks but not others." The status of marriage provides a "'regulative ideal,' an aspiration that shapes purposive activity," even if inevitably parties sometimes fall short of these ideals.[103]

6.2 *Parents and Children*

The contractual dimensions of the marital family involve not only husbands and wives but also parents and children. Summarizing traditional teachings, John Locke, for example, described the natural rights and duties of persons to marry and then conceive and bear children, to nurture, support, protect,

---

100 Marsha Garrison, "Reviving Marriage: Could We? Should We?" *Journal of Law and Family Studies* 10 (2007–2008): 279–335, at 283; see further Marsha Garrison, "Marriage Matters: What's Wrong with the ALI's Domestic Partnership Proposal," in *Reconceiving the Family: Critique on the American Law Institute's Principles of the Law of Family Dissolution*, ed. Robin Fretwell Wilson (New York: Cambridge University Press, 2006), 305–30; and Marsha Garrison, "Toward a Contractarian Account of Family Governance," *Utah Law Review* (1998): 241–69.

101 Scott and Scott, "From Contract to Status"; see further Elizabeth S. Scott and Robert E. Scott, "Marriage as Relational Contract," *Virginia Law Review* 84 (1998): 1225–334.

102 Milton C. Regan, "Calibrated Commitment: The Legal Treatment of Marriage and Cohabitation," *Notre Dame Law Review* 76 (2000–01): 1435–66, at 1439.

103 Ibid., 1463; see further Milton C. Regan Jr., *Family Law and the Pursuit of Intimacy* (New York: NYU Press, 1993); Milton C. Regan Jr., *Alone Together: Law and the Meanings of Marriage* (Oxford: Oxford University Press, 1999).

and educate them, to set them up in their own new homes and vocations, and then to provide them with legacies through last wills and testaments. Children, in turn, had rights to have each of these natural duties discharged—ideally by their natural parents or guardians or, in their absence, by church and state authorities who stood *in loco parentis*.[104] Children's rights have become more clearly differentiated and strongly defended in modern times, albeit with some strong detractors.[105]

Children have not only rights but also duties to their parents, the Western legal tradition has long taught. The great English common lawyer William Blackstone summarized these obligations in classic terms: "The duties of children to their parents arise from a principle of natural justice and retribution. For to those who gave us existence, we naturally owe subjection and obedience during our minority, and honour and reverence ever after; they, who protected the weakness of our infancy, are entitled to our protection in the infirmity of their age; they who by sustenance and education have enabled their offspring to prosper, ought in return to be supported by that offspring, in case they stand in need of assistance. Upon this principle proceed all the duties of children to their parents, which are enjoined by positive laws."[106]

A good number of these traditional children's obligations for parental care and support were absorbed by the twentieth-century welfare state—more so in Western Europe but also in North America. Nonetheless, more than half of the American states have always retained laws obligating children to provide their needy parents with food, clothing, shelter, and medical care and to be accountable for at least some of their parents' bills even after death. These old laws of intergenerational care are getting more attention of late, with the modern welfare state on the fiscal and ideological ropes, not only in the Americas but also in Western Europe. The responsibility of broader family and kin networks for elder care today is an area of intense new academic and public policy discussion, given ever longer life spans and ever shrinking public and private support structures.[107]

104 See sources and discussion in Witte, *Church, State, and Family*, 256–66.

105 Ibid., 238–55.

106 William Blackstone, *Commentaries on the Law of England*, 4 vols. (Oxford: Clarendon Press, 1765), bk. 1, chap. 16.

107 See, for example, sources and discussion in Amy Ziettlow and Naomi Cahn, "The Honor Commandment: Law, Religion, and the Challenge of Elder Care," *Journal of Law and Religion* 30 (2015): 229–59.

7 The Marital Family as a Spiritual Institution

While the marital family is based in part on a contract, it is also more than a mere contract, the Western legal tradition has long taught. United States Supreme Court Justice Joseph Story put this in classic terms:

> Marriage is treated by all civilized nations as a peculiar and favored contract. It is in its origin a contract of natural law.... It is the parent, and not the child of society; it is the source of the city, a sort of seminary of the republic. In civil society it becomes a civil contract, regulated and prescribed by law, and endowed with civil consequences. In most civilized countries, acting under a sense of the force of sacred obligations, it has had the sanctions of religion superadded. It then becomes a religious, as well as a natural and civil contract; for it is a great mistake to suppose, that because it is the one, therefore it may not likewise be the other.[108]

Story cited French philosopher Baron de Montesquieu, who had written that "it is a thing extremely delicate to fix exactly" the line between the temporal and spiritual dimensions of the marital family. For the reality is that "it has happened in all ages and countries, that religion has been blended with marriages. When certain things have been considered as impure or unlawful, and [have] nevertheless become necessary, they were obliged to call in religion to legitimate in the one case, and to reprove in others."[109]

For much of the past two millennia in the West, Christianity helped define these religious or spiritual dimensions of the marital family. In particular, the teaching that marriage is a sacrament or a covenant helped to tie together the diverse natural, social, economic, communicative, and contractual dimensions of family life and attach them to the spiritual pole of the marital family sphere. Christianity was also able to integrate the efforts of various associations and professions that served the marital household, by implementing their theories of subsidiarity and sphere sovereignty that recognized both the irreducibility of the family as a social sphere and the indispensability of the support provided by other institutions, not least the churches and church-based organizations.

---

108 See Joseph Story, *Commentaries on the Conflict of Laws, Foreign and Domestic, In Regard to Contracts, Rights, and Remedies, and Especially in Regard to Marriages, Divorces, Wills, Successions, and Judgments* (Boston: Hilliard Gray & Co., 1834), 100.

109 Baron Montesquieu, *The Spirit of the Laws*, trans. Thomas Nugent (New York: Hafner Publishing Co., 1949 [1748]), 2:67.

In late modern liberal societies, Christianity no longer plays that fully integrating role for all families, though it still does for some church members who accept the church's teachings. Moreover, when Christianity lives up to its family ideals, the church provides secular society with inspirational and aspirational models and teachings of love, charity, and sacrifice for others to emulate. When Christianity abides by its diaconal calling, it provides marital counseling, adoption services, child care and education, and humanitarian aid and emergency relief, particularly for the classic biblical roster of widows, orphans, poor, sojourners, and other *personae miserabiles*. And when Christianity tends to its internal religious legal systems, it provides its members with valuable rules and procedures for marital formation, maintenance, and dissolution as well as family mediation, arbitration, and reconciliation.

7.1 *The Sacrament of Marriage*

For baptized Roman Catholics, who are properly married with the liturgical blessing of the church, marriage is regarded as a sacrament, which embodies and expresses the enduring and mysterious love of Christ and the church. The sacrament of marriage elevates the natural goods of procreation and marital fidelity into a divine act, modeled on the creative act of God the Father in Paradise and the sacrificial act of God the Son, who gave his life and body to the church. The sacrament of marriage also elevates the natural and social dimensions of marriage. Marriage is no longer just a set of biological inclinations and moral instructions for men and women to form enduring and exclusive bonds for the sake of each other and their children. Sacramental marriage is now a channel of divine grace, like baptism, penance, or the Eucharist. Voluntary participation in it brings special divine blessings upon the couple, their children, and the communities of which they are a part. Sacramental marriage is also now a channel of divine work, the means God chose not only to perpetuate the human species but also to preserve the church. As Pope John Paul II put it, "The future of the world, and of the church, passes through the family."[110]

This idea of the sacrament of marriage is rooted in Ephesians 5:21–32, which compares the mutually sacrificial relations of husband and wife to the "mysterious" bond between Christ and the church.

110 Pope John Paul II, *Familiaris Consortio* (On the Role of the Christian Family in the Modern World), item 75 available at http://w2.vatican.va/content/john-paul-ii/en/apost_exhortations/documents/hf_jp-ii_exh_19811122_familiaris-consortio.html. See further Robert P. George and Gerard V. Bradley, "Pope John Paul II," in Witte and Hauk, *Christianity and Family Law*, 363–80.

> Submit to one another out of reverence for Christ. Wives, submit yourselves to your own husbands as you do to the Lord. For the husband is the head of the wife as Christ is the head of the church, his body, of which he is the Savior. Now as the church submits to Christ, so also wives should submit to their husbands in everything. Husbands, love your wives, just as Christ loved the church and gave himself up for her to make her holy, cleansing her by the washing with water through the word, and to present her to himself as a radiant church, without stain or wrinkle or any other blemish, but holy and blameless. In this same way, husbands ought to love their wives as their own bodies. He who loves his wife loves himself. After all, no one ever hated their own body, but they feed and care for their body, just as Christ does the church—for we are members of his body. "For this reason a man will leave his father and mother and be united to his wife, and the two will become one flesh." This is a profound mystery [*mysterion; sacramentum*]—but I am talking about Christ and the church. However, each one of you also must love his wife as he loves himself, and the wife must respect her husband.

In a brilliant and massive study, Philip Reynolds has traced the idea of the marital sacrament from pre-Christian sources all the way to its final canonical formulation by the Catholic Church in 1563.[111] In the decree *Tametsi*, the Council of Trent for the first time declared canonically that marriage is one of the seven canonical sacraments of the church; indeed, marriage is the first sacrament, instituted by God at creation and symbolized by Christ's union with the church. Weaving together the familiar texts of Genesis 1–2 and Ephesians 5, the Council of Trent declared:

> The perpetual and indissoluble bond of matrimony was expressed by the first parent of the human race, when, under the influence of the divine Spirit, he said: This now is bone of my bones and flesh of my flesh. Wherefore a man shall leave his father and mother and shall cleave to his wife, and they shall be two in one flesh. But that by this bond two only are united and joined together, Christ the Lord taught more plainly when referring to those last words, as having been spoken by God, he said: Therefore now they are not two, but one flesh, and immediately ratified the firmness of the bond.

111 Philip L. Reynolds, *How Marriage Became One of the Sacraments* (Cambridge: Cambridge University Press, 2016).

> But the grace which was to perfect the natural love, and confirm that indissoluble union, and sanctify the persons married, Christ Himself, the instituter and perfecter of the venerable sacraments, merited for us by His passion, which Paul the Apostle intimates when he says: "Husbands love your wives, as Christ also loved the Church, and delivered himself up for it"; adding immediately: "This is a great sacrament, but I speak in Christ and in the Church."
>
> Since therefore matrimony in the evangelical law surpasses in grace through Christ the ancient marriages, our holy Fathers, the councils, and the tradition of the universal Church, have with good reason always taught that it is to be numbered among the sacraments of the New Law.[112]

This idea of the marital sacrament pervades Roman Catholic teaching to this day. The Second Vatican Council (1962–65) elaborated the implications of this sacramental theology for the natural, social, economic, communicative, and contractual dimensions of the family sphere. The church constitution *Gaudium et Spes*, for example, declared:

> God Himself is the author of matrimony, endowed as it is with various benefits and purposes. All of these have a very decisive bearing on the continuation of the human race, on the personal development and eternal destiny of the individual members of a family, and on the dignity, stability, peace, and prosperity of the family itself and of human society as a whole.[113]

"The well-being of ... society is intimately linked with the healthy condition of that community produced by marriage and family," *Gaudium et spes* continued. "The family is a kind of school of deeper humanity," holding out a model, method, and medium of love, authority, dignity, faithfulness, education, nurture, discipline, and care for each new generation of children to learn, and for other institutions to emulate.

> Thus the family is the foundation of society. In it the various generations come together and help one another to grow wiser and to harmonize personal rights with the other requirements of social life. All those, therefore,

---

112 In H.J. Schroeder, ed., *Councils and Decrees of the Council of Trent* (St. Louis: B. Herder Book Co., 1941), 180.

113 In Walter M. Abbott and Joseph Gallagher, ed. and trans., *The Documents of Vatican II* (New York: Guild Press, 1966), 199, 250.

> who exercise influence over communities and social groups should work effectively for the welfare of marriage and the family. Public authority should regard it as a sacred duty to recognize, protect, and promote their authentic nature, to shield public morality, and to favor the prosperity of domestic life.[114]

The Council declared elsewhere, "The family is, so to speak, the domestic Church." Parents are "the first preachers" who nurture the faith, hope, and charity not only of their children but of broader society as well.[115]

Gaudium et Spes was even more expansive in its treatment of marital love as indispensable to the "well-being of the individual person" and to the integration of the classic marital goods of faith, children, and sacrament:

> The intimate partnership of married life and love has been established by the Creator and qualified by His laws. It is rooted in the conjugal covenant of irrevocable personal consent.... [A] man and a woman, who by the marriage covenant of conjugal love "are no longer two, but one flesh" (Mt. 19:6), ... experience the meaning of their oneness and attain to it with growing perfection day by day. As a mutual gift of two persons, this intimate union, as well as the good of the children, imposes total fidelity on the spouses and argues for an unbreakable oneness between them. Christ the Lord abundantly blessed this many-faceted love, ... [f]or as God of old made Himself present to His people through a covenant of love and fidelity, so now the Savior of men and the Spouse of the Church comes into the lives of married Christians through the sacrament of matrimony.[116]

Marital love involves "the good of the whole person ... [which] ennobles ... those special ingredients and signs of the friendship distinctive of marriage." Marital love impels spouses to make "a free and mutual gift of themselves, a gift proving itself by gentle affection and by deed." It is expressed in sexual intercourse, which is a "good," "noble," and "worthy" form of community and communication. It is structured through the "equal personal dignity of wife and husband, a dignity acknowledged by mutual and total love." And marital

114 Ibid., 249, 257.

115 *Lumen Gentium*, in Abbott and Gallagher, *The Documents of Vatican II*, 14, 29. On the family as "domestic church," see Lisa Sowle Cahill, *Family: A Christian Social Perspective* (Minneapolis: Fortress Press, 2000).

116 *Gaudium et Spes*, 249–51.

love brings to the couple the "cultural, psychological, and social renewal" that they need daily to survive, flourish, and indeed to "perfect" themselves.[117]

In an appendix to *Gaudium et Spes*, the Council elaborated the teaching that marriage is "a covenant of love":

> Marital consent of its essence intends the unity of this covenant, its indissolubility and the love that is devoted to the service of life. The stronger and purer the marital love, the more strongly and perseveringly will the spouses accept and realize marriage's specific traits and its essential goods.... No one is aware of how seriously necessary it is that love be fully present in the act of consent, and increase throughout the entire married life. For love will fulfill and cause to be fulfilled what the consent has said and has promised.[118]

A number of subsequent church documents have echoed and elaborated the Second Vatican Council's integrative theory of the marital family sphere, now with attention to the role of other social institutions as well.[119] The 1968 *Catechism* of the Catholic Church, for example, called on both husbands and wives to live in "authentic dignity of persons, be joined to one another in equal affection, harmony of mind, and the work of mutual sanctification," and "by the sacrifices and joys of their vocation and through faithful love" testify to "the mystery of love which the Lord revealed to the world." The *Catechism* also called on a plurality of institutions to serve and aid the marital family so constituted, just as the family as a vital social unit serves and aids society and its members. The church and its theologians, ethicists, and other masters of "the sacred sciences" should aid marital couples through their pastoral care, special worship and liturgies, and catechesis of children and counseling of couples. The state should "give due attention to the needs of the family regarding housing, the education of children, working conditions, social security and taxes," and, through immigration reforms, ensure "migrants their right to live together as a family." The "medical, biological, social, and psychological" sciences should "pool their efforts" to advance "the welfare of marriage and the family," particularly in procreation and child care.[120] This idea of "subsidiarity,"

117 Ibid., 251–53.

118 Quoted in Theodore Mackin, *What is Marriage?* (New York: Paulist Press, 1982), 261.

119 See samples in Austin Flannery, ed., *Vatican Council II: Volume 2, More Postconciliar Documents*, new rev. ed. (Dublin: New Dominican Publication, 1998), and discussion in Richard M. Hogan and John M. Levoir, *Covenant of Love: Pope John Paul II on Sexuality, Marriage and Family in the Modern World* (Garden City, NY: Doubleday, 1985).

120 *The Catechism of Modern Man* (Boston: Daughters of St. Paul, 1968), 572–76.

that marriage requires the aid, the *subsidium*, of multiple institutions for its guidance and effective functioning, is an important insight into the reality that the marital family is a multidimensional and multi-institutional association. And it reflects Vatican II's teaching that democratic states that respect the religious freedom of all citizens have authority to maintain just state family laws that are binding on Catholic and non-Catholic faithful alike.[121]

Equally important to the modern Catholic integrative understanding of the marital family was the 1983 Code of Canon Law.[122] The Code again described marriage as a "covenant" as well as a "sacrament." It did not treat procreation as the primary good of marriage, as *Humanae Vitae* (1968) and other earlier statements had done, but it called for a balance among the goods of fidelity, children, and sacrament.[123] And the Code spurned traditional doctrines of male headship within the home, calling both parents to sacrificial love for each other and their children. "[E]ach of the spouses has equal obligations and rights to those things which pertain to the partnership of conjugal life." Moreover, fathers and mothers together "have the most serious duty and the primary right to do all in their power to see to the physical, social, cultural, moral, and religious upbringing of their children."[124] These egalitarian lessons of spousal and parental relations have been further driven home in an impressive series of recent Catholic handbooks, pamphlets, illustrated sermons, storybooks, websites, and learned but accessible volumes on marriage preparation, household management, spousal relations, Christian parentage, childrearing, elder care, and intergenerational responsibility.[125]

7.2 *The Covenant of Marriage*

The recent Catholic emphasis on the "marital covenant" alongside the "marital sacrament" holds important ecumenical and interdisciplinary promise. For the

121 See, for example, Russell Hittinger, "Society, Subsidiarity, and Authority in Catholic Social Thought," in *Civilizing Authority: Society, State, and Church*, ed. Patrick M. Brennan (Lanham, MD: Lexington Books, 2007), 119–44; Michelle Evans and Augusto Zimmermann, eds., *Global Perspectives on Subsidiarity* (Dordrecht: Springer, 2014).

122 *Code of Canon Law: Latin-English Translation* (London: Collins, 1983), Canons 1055–65. See also ibid., Canons 1425, 1432, 1490, 1671–715.

123 Ibid., Canons 1055, 1134. See also *Code of Canons of the Eastern Churches: New English Translation* (Washington, DC: Canon Law Society of America, 1998 [1983]), Canon 776 on "the matrimonial covenant."

124 *Code of Canon Law*, Canons 1055, 1134–36. See Lisa Sowle Cahill, *Sex, Gender and Christian Ethics* (Cambridge: Cambridge University Press, 1991).

125 See, for example, Cahill, *Family: A Christian Social Perspective*; John F. Kippley, *Sex and the Marriage Covenant: A Basis for Morality* (Cincinnati, OH: CCL, 1991); and Julie Hanlon Rubio, *A Christian Theology of Marriage and Family* (New York: Paulist Press, 2003).

metaphor of marital covenant bridges not only formulations from the Hebrew Bible and the New Testament but also theological and legal, religious and secular, natural-law and theological discourses on marriage and family life. And it appeals to analogous understandings of the spiritual dimensions of the marital family among the world religions.[126]

Early Protestants like Heinrich Bullinger and John Calvin first emphasized the biblical teachings on the marital covenant and their implications for state family law. It is worth excavating these biblical teachings a bit more in explicating one formative way of thinking about the spiritual dimension of the marital family and how that dimension relates to others.[127]

The Hebrew Bible relates that God entered a special covenant with the people of Israel, building on earlier covenantal promises to Noah and Abraham. In this new covenant, God promised Israel divine favor and blessing in return for obedience to God's law. But God also threatened divine condemnation and punishment if the people disobeyed the law and worshipped other gods.[128] In the Bible's understanding of covenant, both sides yield a portion of their natural freedom to each other and agree to limit and direct their actions in accordance with the terms of their covenant. Both sides agree on the dire consequences to them and their descendants for noncompliance with the covenant. In the ancient world, peace treaties and alliances between tribes and peoples were sometimes formed by covenants of this sort. Their formation often featured elaborate ceremonies and sacrifices, communal oath-swearing, and the erection or dedication of a physical marker signifying the covenant and sometimes recording its terms.[129] Covenants were presumptively permanent, but they were mutable and conditional and could end when fundamentally betrayed. This was the special covenantal relationship between God and Israel. Moses's charge to Israel in Deuteronomy, as part of an elaborate public recitation and ceremony, was one of several confirmations of this covenant:

126 See sources in John Witte, Jr. and Eliza Ellison, eds., *Covenant Marriage in Comparative Perspective* (Grand Rapids, MI: Eerdmans 2005).

127 This section is distilled from John Witte, Jr., "The Covenant of Marriage: Its Biblical Roots, Historical Influence, and Modern Uses," *INTAMS Review on Marriage and Spirituality* 18 (2012): 147–65.

128 Genesis 9:8–19; 15:1–6, 18; 17:2; 22:16–18.

129 See Daniel J. Elazar, *Covenant and Polity in Biblical Israel: Biblical Foundations and Jewish Expressions* (London: Transaction Publishers, 1998), 163; and Delbert R. Hillers, *Covenant: The History of a Biblical Idea* (Baltimore, MD: Johns Hopkins University Press, 1969), 25–39.

> This very day, the Lord your God is commanding you to observe these statutes and ordinances: so observe them diligently with all your heart and with all your soul. Today you have obtained the Lord's agreement: to be your God; and for you to walk in his ways, to keep his statutes, his commandments, and his ordinances and to obey him. Today the Lord has obtained your agreement: to be his treasured people, as he promised you, and to keep his commandments; for him to set you high above all nations that he has made, in praise and in fame and in honor; for you to be a people holy to the Lord your God, as he promised.[130]

The Hebrew prophets Hosea, Jeremiah, Ezekiel, Isaiah, and Malachi all analogized this covenantal relationship between God and Israel to the marital relationship between a husband and wife. Just as God chose to give up his divine freedom to be bound to the people of Israel, the prophets argued, so a man chooses to give up his natural freedom to bind himself to his wife, to become "one flesh" with her. Just as God spent time courting Israel and lavishing her with gifts and attention after conversing with their founding father, Abraham, so a man spends his time courting his potential wife after consulting with her father or guardian. Just as Israel chose Yahweh out of all the ancient pantheon to be its God and to make sacrifices only to this God, so a woman chooses her husband from all the other men in the universe to be her only husband, and to dedicate herself to him alone. Just as God and Israel bound themselves together by a special covenant, each promising to be faithful and obedient to the other, so a husband and wife swear to a special marital covenant, each promising faith and obedience to the other in accordance with their agreement and with the laws of God. Just as a breach of the divine covenant between God and Israel will hurt both parties and have devastating consequences for later generations, so a breach of a marital covenant will hurt the innocent spouse and children. The Old Testament prophets devoted several long chapters to this marriage metaphor, depicting graphically God's courtship and marriage to Israel, his dismay at her "playing the harlot" with other gods, his suit against Israel in a divorce court, and then his reconciliation with Israel, if for no other reason than protecting the children.[131]

130 Deuteronomy 26:16–19 (NRSV); see further Deuteronomy 29:13; Exodus 6:7; Leviticus 26:12.

131 Hosea 2:2–23; Isaiah 1:21–22; 54:5–8; 57:3–10; 61:10–11; 62:4–5; Jeremiah 2:2–3; 3:1–25; 13:27; 23:10; 31:32; Ezekiel 16:1–63; 23:1–49; Malachi 1–2 and analysis in Gordon P. Hugenberger, *Marriage as Covenant: A Study of Biblical Law and Ethics Governing Marriage Developed from the Perspective of Malachi* (Leiden: Brill, 1994); Michael G. Lawler, "Marriage as Covenant in the Catholic Tradition," in Witte and Ellison, *Covenant Marriage*, 70–92.

All these prophets used the metaphor of covenantal marriage in part for anthropomorphic reasons. By casting in graphic human and emotional terms that everyone could understand what it must feel like to God to be betrayed by the beloved chosen people, the prophets hoped to shake the wayward people from sin and bring them back to faithfulness.

The Prophet Malachi, however, called each human marriage a special covenant, indeed an echo and expression of God's loving covenant with Israel. He urged his readers to be faithful to their covenantal marriage with each other, just as God had been faithful in covenantal relationship with Israel. And Malachi equated the breach of the marital covenant with breach of the broader covenant with God, which God will punish. Malachi 2:13–16 provides:

> You cover the Lord's altar with tears, with weeping and groaning because he no longer regards the offering and accepts it with favor at your hand. You ask, "Why does he not?" Because the Lord was witness to the covenant between you and the wife of your youth, to whom you have been faithless, though she is your companion and your wife by covenant. Has not the one God made and sustained for us the spirit of life? And what does he desire? Godly offspring. So take heed to yourselves, and let none be faithless to the wife of his youth. "For I hate divorce, says the Lord the God of Israel, and covering one's garments with violence, says the Lord, the God of hosts. So take heed to yourselves and do not be faithless."

There is a lot packed into this passage, and it has long been an exegetical battleground.[132] Most important for our purposes is how the prophets' metaphor of marital covenant holds valuable lessons for human marriages and families. First, the metaphor confirms the created form of marriage as a monogamous union between one man and one woman. Even God, who had the perfect right to pick many brides, chose only one, beloved Israel, with whom to produce godly descendants. The Malachi 2 passage, just quoted, ties this norm directly to the primordial creation story of Genesis 1–2. At creation, God could have created two or more wives for Adam but chose "to breathe his spirit" into just one wife, even though God had ample spiritual residue to give life to many more wives. God could have created three or four types of humans to be the image of God, but he created two: male and female.[133] In the law, God could

132 See, for example, Sharon Moughtin-Mumby, *Sexual and Marital Metaphors in Hosea, Jeremiah, Isaiah, and Ezekiel* (Oxford: Oxford University Press, 2008); and Paul F. Palmer, "Christian Marriage: Contract or Covenant," *Theological Studies* 33 (1972), 617–65.

133 Genesis 1:27.

have commanded Israel to worship two or more gods but restricted them to one. Marriage, as an order of creation and a symbol of God's special relationship with the elect, involves two parties and two parties only.

Second, the covenant metaphor confirms that God participates in each marriage. The passage in Malachi again underscores this, echoing the Genesis story of creation. Just as God gave the first man, Adam, and the first woman, Eve, "the spirit of life" and brought them together, so God gives each man and woman a spirit of love and witnesses and solemnizes their union. God is not only the creator of the institution of marriage, Malachi makes clear. God is also the "witness" to each marriage; God's presence and testimony legitimate each new marital covenant that follows prescribed forms and norms. God is also the guarantor of the marriage, on whom the couple can call to ensure that the terms of the marital agreement are fulfilled. And God is the exemplar of a faithful covenantal marriage, as shown in the metaphorical covenantal marriage of God with Israel. To enter a marriage, the prophets teach, is to enter a new relationship not only with one's spouse but also with God. God may be present in that marital relationship in various ways, the later Christian tradition taught—through parents, peers, or pastors who represent divine authority and priesthood, through neighbors, congregants, and community members who represent divine hospitality and support, or through children, grandchildren, or kinfolk who represent God's gifts and blessings. But the main point is that marriage is a special creation of God, supported by a whole network of relationships by which God is present.

Third, the metaphor of covenant confirms the divinely ordained procreative function of marriage. Even God, who had the power to create many faithful followers for many generations, chose instead to produce "godly seed" through the chosen bride Israel under the normative terms of the covenant. This, too, echoes the creation story, where God delegates to Adam and Eve the power of creating and cultivating the next generation of human image-bearers of God, telling them to "be fruitful and multiply" and fill the earth. Covenantal marriage underscores this ordained procreative purpose of marriage. But the metaphor also makes clear, as Malachi highlights, that faithful married couples are called to produce not just any children but "godly offspring," the next generation of God's covenant faithful who love God and live by the laws of God's covenant. The marital covenant makes procreation an extraordinary responsibility. It is a sharing with God in the creation and nurture of a new image-bearer and a new covenant-follower of God on earth, a responsibility that stays with parents for as long as they and their children live.

Fourth, the covenant metaphor confirms the divine laws governing marriage formation set out in both the Mosaic law and the natural law revealed prior to Moses to all humanity. Even God, who had the perfect right to take any bride by any means he wished, obeys his own laws for proper courtship and marriage. God chooses a spouse carefully and takes time in courting her. God seeks her consent and that of her father, Abraham, then provides her with engagement and wedding gifts, and rehearses for her the terms of the marital covenant before their wedding day, so that they both understand what they are getting into. The couple then celebrate their covenantal union in an elaborate public ceremony and public exchange of vows before the whole community with an authorized official, Moses, presiding. The metaphorical story of God's covenantal marriage with Israel, as told by the prophets, cleverly underscores the very Mosaic laws of marriage that the covenanted people of Israel were required to follow in forming their own marriages.

Fifth, the metaphor of covenant makes clear that each individual marital covenant is part and product of a much larger covenantal relationship between God and humanity. Both the husband and the wife must be faithful to this covenant, Malachi makes clear. This is a new egalitarian ethic. The earlier prophets, echoing the Genesis account of humanity's fall into sin through the failings of Eve, had always focused on Israel, the wayward wife, the adulteress, who had gone after other gods, producing illegitimate children, who could not be supported but must "die out."[134] That image of the fallen woman comes through as late as Proverbs 2:17, a book produced a century before the Book of Malachi: "You will be saved from the loose woman, from the adventuress with her smooth words, who forsakes the companion of her youth, and forgets the covenant of her God."

Malachi turned the tables and focused on the husband, too, calling him to be faithful to his wife, just as God is faithful to Israel. For a husband to wander after another woman—whether a lover, prostitute, or concubine—is now not just an act of adultery but an act of blasphemy, an insult to the divine example of covenantal marriage that God, the metaphorical husband, offers to each human husband living under God's covenant. Husbands are now to follow God's example of offering "covenant love" (*chesed*) to their wives, remaining faithful to them even in the face of "violence," trouble, or betrayal. Husbands are also to follow God's example in living both by the letter and by the spirit of the traditional law of divorce. There is still a place for divorce in cases of deep rupture of the relationship. "God hates divorce," Malachi says, but God does not prohibit it. Instead, God calls husbands not to divorce lightly on grounds of mere "uncleanness" (as Deuteronomy 24 put it), nor to divorce harshly, "covering their garments with violence" (as Malachi 2 put it). To breach one's marital

134 Hosea 2:4–5; Sirach 23:24–26; Wisdom 3:16–17, 4:16.

covenant lightly or violently, Malachi teaches, is tantamount to breaching one's covenant with God. For those who do so, God "no longer regards or accepts" their offerings or worship—a sure sign of divine condemnation. In Malachi's formulation, marriage has now become a part of one's religious duty, a part of living in covenantal community, a part of one's expression of true love (*chesed*) of God, neighbor, and self.[135]

Christians over the centuries have incorporated these covenantal ideals and elements of marriage and family into the personal ethics of believers and into the spiritual lives of the church community. The many biblical passages on the marital covenant have provided endless inspiration for sermons, catechisms, confessional and pastoral handbooks, and many other forms of moral instruction for family life that remain in place in Christian communities to this day. Moreover, Christians translated these covenantal ideals into internal religious norms for church discipline and external civil norms for the state and broader society. These ideas helped inform the Anglo-American common-law teaching of the "status" of marriage with its preset terms, conditions, and expected performance, and they help explain why common-law statutes and cases often speak of the "marital covenant."[136] Today, a few American states offer prospective couples "covenant marriage" options, reflecting these traditional forms and norms as an alternative to the "contract marriage" option available in all states.

Concluding Reflections: the Modern Marital Family in Traditional Christian and Modern Liberal Perspectives

This little volume has retrieved and reconstructed traditional Western teachings about the integrated marital family sphere and shown their echoes and elaborations in various circles of scholarly discourse about sex, marriage, and family today. I have used the metaphor of the marital family sphere—with natural and spiritual poles and with various social, economic, communicative, and contractual dimensions radiating between them. This sphere metaphor is a heuristic devise—a picture to describe the various dimensions of marital family life, the different disciplinary perspectives on the family gathered

135 Edward Schillebeeckx, *Marriage: Secular Reality and Saving Mystery* (London: Sheed and Ward, 1965), 64.

136 See sources and discussion in Witte, *Church, State, and Family*, 72–105, 310–15.

around these perspectives, and the range of institutions and professions that have interacted with the marital family historically and today.

Western writers over the centuries have often used what Don Browning aptly called a "double language" in describing the marital family sphere—a common philosophical or rational language and a specialized theological or confessional language.[137] When they work up from the bottom natural pole of the marital family sphere, these scholars often use philosophical language to describe the natural qualities of the economic, social, communicative, and contractual dimensions of the marital family. They talk, for example, about "bio-economic" or "natural-material" dimensions of marriage or of marital communication, or the "natural" rights and duties attached to the contract or status of marriage and parentage. Often this philosophical language had early expression in Judaism, Greek philosophy, and Roman law, later elaboration in Christian natural law and jurisprudential traditions, and further echoes and elaborations in post-Christian Enlightenment philosophical and legal movements that helped form modern liberalism.

By contrast, when they work down from the top spiritual or transcendent pole of the sphere, religious scholars often use more specialized theological terms like the marital sacrament or marital covenant. This theological language also seeks to describe and integrate the economic, social, communicative, and contractual dimensions of the marital family, and it generally confirms what nature and its philosophical expositions teach. But the theological accounts of marriage as a covenant or sacrament also aim to enhance each of these dimensions of the marital family, "spiritualizing" and integrating them into a framework that treats the marital family as a presumptively permanent, loving, enduring, and sacrificial union designed to perpetuate and to emulate the creative, sacrificial, and pedagogical activities of God.[138]

Christianity rarely plays that full integrative and spiritualizing role for family life and law in the West today—in part because Christianity has lost much of its cultural potency and legal influence in the West. The "pressures of modernization," as Don Browning calls them, have put the family and various other social spheres into ever sharper competition, often distorting and

137 Don S. Browning, *Equality and the Family: A Fundamental, Practical Theology of Children, Mothers, and Fathers in Modern Society* (Grand Rapids, MI: Eerdmans, 2007), 211; and Don S. Browning, *Marriage and Modernization: How Globalization Threatens Marriage and What to do about It* (Grand Rapids, MI: Eerdmans, 2003), 130.

138 See Rafael Domingo and Gonzalo Rodríguez-Fraile Díaz, *Spiritualizing Humanity* (n.p., 2022); and Rafael Domingo, "Body, Soul, and Spirit of the Law: Toward a Holistic Legal Paradigm," *Oxford Journal of Law and Religion* 7 (2018): 230–49.

dividing various dimensions of the family in the process.[139] More and more, the *natural* and the bio-economic dimensions of the marital family have been split apart by the specialized offerings, interventions, and collusions of financial and biomedical market spheres. More and more, the *social* dimensions of marriage and family life—the value and utility of the marital household for reproduction, for socializing children, for curbing promiscuity, for ongoing mutual nurture and support—have been reduced to discretionary and often transient matters of private ordering, with the state and society often left to bear the costs of childrearing in the event of dissolution. More and more, the *economic* forces of markets, technology, advertising, and labor demands have encroached so deeply into the marital family sphere that it often can no longer perform its customary tasks or hold its traditional attraction. More and more, modern societies have relegated the *contractual* dimensions of marriage to state law alone, which now operates as an increasingly dominant, if not autonomous, cultural force rather than as one institution alongside the church, family, and other institutions. As the *communicative* aspects of marriage have become more important, entire professions of marriage educators and psychotherapists have arisen to improve skills in handling marital strains, replacing the latent communicative contributions of folk wisdom and religious institutions. And the ritual element of the communicative dimension has either been increasingly narrowed to the formalities of courthouse ceremonies or expanded to television entertainment extravaganzas that have little to do with the religious communal drama that once attended the formation of a marriage.

These separations of the different dimensions of marriage are related to the new separations of the modern sexual field noted in the introduction to this publication: the separations between marriage and sex; between marriage and childbirth; between marriage and childrearing; between childbirth and parenting; between sex and physical contact (with the advent of the virtual world); and between sexual intercourse, childbirth, and biological filiation (with the introduction of in vitro fertilization, surrogacy, and sperm banks).

Traditionally in the West, both Christian family theory and state family law worked hard to prevent such separations—albeit, of course, never perfectly. They promoted the integration of marriage, sexual intercourse, childbirth, and childrearing and prohibited harmful sexual activities like fornication, prostitution, concubinage, adultery, desertion, polygamy, and no-fault divorce. This position now stands in marked contrast to much contemporary family law and theory that accommodates, and sometimes advocates, the separations of

139 Browning, *Marriage and Modernization.*

the sexual field using the new constitutional logic of sexual liberty, privacy, and autonomy. It is a telling anecdote that the latest American Law Institute restatement on family law is labeled *Principles of the Law of Family Dissolution*, and the latest Canadian restatement on point is titled *Beyond Conjugality*.[140]

The escalating breakdown of the marital family in modern Western liberal lands in the last half century has caused massive harm to women and children, and to minority and poor communities around the United States and other Western countries. To be sure, some 90 percent of American citizens with college educations and sufficient means now form stable marital families and raise their children in intact homes, giving these children much higher probabilities of success. These are much stronger numbers than a generation or two ago, when divorce rates in this same population approached 50 percent.[141] But persons with fewer means and less education today "have all but given up on marriage," June Carbone and Naomi Cahn write, in an impressive but sobering new demographic study about the state of the modern American family. "For the majority of Americans who haven't graduated from college, marriage rates are low, divorce rates are high, and a first child is more likely to be born to parents who are single than to parents who are married."[142] And the numbers of nonmarital cohabitation and procreation are considerably higher in most parts of Europe, even while many European nations are losing the cultural cohesion, political will, and economic capital needed to maintain the welfare state that, for the past century, has absorbed many of the responsibilities historically discharged by the marital family.[143]

Happily, in recent decades a whole cadre of leading scholars, public policy and public health experts, and various cultural and political leaders,

---

140 See Wilson, *Reconceiving the Family*; Daniel Cere, "Canadian Conjugal Mosaic: From Multiculturalism to Multiconjugalism?" in *Marriage and Divorce in a Multi-Cultural Context: Multi-Tiered Marriage and the Boundaries of Civil Law and Religion*, ed. Joel A. Nichols (Cambridge: Cambridge University Press, 2011), 284–308.

141 See detailed annual statistics and analysis by the National Marriage Project at the University of Virginia http://nationalmarriageproject.org/ and the Institute for American Values, http://www.americanvalues.org/.

142 June Carbone and Naomi Cahn, *Marriage Matters: How Inequality is Remaking the American Family* (Oxford: Oxford University Press, 2014), 19–20. See further Maureen Baker and Vivienne Elizabeth, *Marriage in an Age of Cohabitation* (Oxford: Oxford University Press, 2014); Laura M. Tach and Alicia Eads, "Trends in the Economic Consequences of Marital and Cohabitational Dissolution in the United States," *Demography* 52 (2015): 401–32; Gillian Douglas, "Marriage, Cohabitation, and Parentage—From Contract to Status?" in *Cross Currents: Family Law and Politcy in the US and England*, ed. Sanford N. Katz, John Eekelaar, and Mavis Maclean (Oxford: Oxford University Press, 2000), 211–33.

143 See sources and discussion in Witte, *Church, State, and Family*, 306–10, 336–41.

conservative and liberal, religious and secular alike, are responding decisively to this crisis of modern family life, even if their efforts are sometimes lampooned in some quarters. This pro-family movement has sought to combine traditional family teachings and modern social science and public-health findings to advocate for stable marital families, responsible sex and parentage, and proper family planning as essential for private flourishing and social stability. And this movement has pressed for robust new church, state, and economic policies in support of stable marital families and households—including, notably, same-sex marital families.

My contribution to this pro-family movement over the years and in this volume has been to show the overlapping consensus and creative convergences between traditional Western teachings on sex, marriage, and family life and modern liberal teachings on sexual privacy, equality, and domestic autonomy. While recognizing that some "modern liberties" and "traditional family values" cannot be easily reconciled—abortion is a poignant example—I have argued that there is more overlapping consensus on sex, marriage, and family life between them than we often realize. That overlapping consensus was clear when classical liberalism first came to prominent and eventually predominant expression in Western lands and laws in place of traditional Christian teachings. Nonetheless, many of the greatest architects of Western liberalism from 1650 to 1900—John Locke, Baron Montesquieu, Mary Wollstonecraft, Frances Hutcheson, David Hume, Adam Smith, William Paley, Jeremy Bentham, John Adams, Thomas Jefferson, and others—embraced many traditional teachings and laws on sex, marriage, and family life, often using new logics to support old practices. This overlapping consensus can also be seen anew in the recent battles over same-sex marriage, where many advocates have sought to extend the private and public goods of marriage and stable family life to same-sex families, often using old logics to support new practices.

It is worth reflecting on these two moments of overlapping consensus and creative convergence between traditional Christian teachings on the marital family and classical and modern liberal teachings respectively.[144] I first take up the early modern story where these two sets of teachings were ultimately reconciled, and then suggest pathways for how the recent battles over same-sex marriage might ultimately help support the law and culture and the marital family sphere.

144 For the next several paragraphs, see sources and discussion in ibid., 151–83.

Traditional Teachings and Classical Liberalism

From various perspectives, Enlightenment liberal writers embraced and enhanced the configuration of marriage and family life that had been adumbrated by Aristotle, elaborated by Aquinas and the medieval schoolmen, and echoed by sundry early modern Catholics and Protestants alike. This argument started with several basic realities about human nature and sexual reproduction. First, unlike most other animals, humans crave sex all the time, especially when they are young and most fertile. They don't have a short rutting or mating season, followed by a long period of sexual quietude. Second, unlike most other animals, human babies are born weak, fragile, and utterly dependent for many years. They are not ready to run, swim, or fly away upon birth or shortly thereafter. They need protection, food, shelter, clothing, and education. Most human mothers have a hard time caring fully for their children on their own, especially if they already have several others. They need help, especially from the fathers and their kin networks. Third, however, most human fathers will bond and help with a child only if they are certain of their paternity. Put a baby cradle in a public place, and most women will stop out of natural empathy. Most men will walk by, unless they are unusually charitable or are deputized to give care. Once assured of their paternity, however, most men will bond deeply with their children, help with their care and support, and defend them at great sacrifice. For they will see their children as a continuation and extension of themselves, of their name, property, and teachings, of their genes, we now say. Fourth, unlike virtually all other higher animals, humans have the freedom and the capacity to engage in destructive behavior in pursuit of their own sexual gratification. Given the lower risks and costs to them, men have historically been more prone to extramarital sex than women, exploiting prostitutes, concubines, impoverished women, and servant girls in so doing and yielding a perennial underclass of "bastards" who have always fared poorly.

Given these four factors, this traditional argument went, rational human beings and societies have learned, often by cruel and hard experience, to develop enduring and exclusive sexual relationships, eventually called marriages, as the best form and forum of sexual bonding and reproductive success. Stable monogamous marriages are designed to provide for the ongoing sexual needs and desires of a husband and wife. They ensure that both fathers and mothers are certain that a baby born to them is theirs. They ensure that husband and wife will together care for, nurture, and educate their children until they mature. And they deter both spouses from destructive sexual behavior outside the home.

Echoing some parts of the Christian tradition, Enlightenment liberal writers encouraged husbands and wives to work hard to maintain active and healthy sex lives—even when, indeed especially when, procreation was not possible. Robust sexual communication within marriage, they argued, is essential for couples to deepen their marital love and to remain in their own marital beds, rather than testing their neighbor's. And marital sex sometimes is even more important when the marital home is (newly) empty and husbands and wives depend more centrally on each other (not on their children) for emotional confirmation and fulfillment. Not every sexual act within the marital bed needs to be procreative. Sexual intimacy between married couples is an essential good in its own right, regardless of procreative intent, capacity, or result.

Enlightenment liberal writers further emphasized that parents and children have reciprocal natural rights and natural duties. They emphasized the vital organic bonds between mother, father, and child and stipulated that the man and woman who produce a child should have the prima facie right and duty to care for that child. They emphasized that children have the correlative right to be raised, if possible, by the parents who procreate them—or adopt them. And they emphasized that exclusive and enduring monogamous marriages are the best way to ensure that men and women are treated with equal dignity and respect, and that husbands and wives, and parents and children, provide each other with mutual support and protection throughout their lifetimes and through their estates thereafter.

Finally, Enlightenment liberal writers warned against sexual activities and interactions that jeopardized the stability and support of the marital family, and the rights and liberties of its members. Polygyny was out because it fractures marital trust and troth, harms wives and children, privileges patriarchy and sexual slavery, and foments male lust and adultery. Polyandry was out because it creates paternal uncertainty and catalyzes male rivalry to the ultimate detriment of the children. Incest was out because it overrides the instincts of natural revulsion, it weakens bloodlines, and it deters the creation of new kinship networks which are essential for civil society and political coherence. Prostitution and fornication were out because they often exploit women, foster libertinism, deter marriage, and produce vulnerable non-marital children who becomes wards of church, state, and society. Adultery was out for some of the same reasons, but even more because it shatters marital fidelity and trust, diffuses family resources and parental energy, and risks sexual disease and physical retaliation of the betrayed spouse. Easy divorce was out because it erodes marital fidelity and investment, jeopardizes long-term spousal support and care, and squanders family property on which children eventually depend to care for their elderly parents. By the turn of the twentieth century, similar natural rights arguments were being used to begin to stamp out the discrimination that the law still retained against spinsters, wives, and nonmarital children.

Enlightenment liberal writers pressed their arguments for traditional Western family and sexual norms using a surfeit of arguments from nature, reason, custom, fairness, prudence, utility, pragmatism, and common sense. Some of these Enlightenment writers were inspired, no doubt, by their personal Christian faith, others by a conservative desire to maintain the status quo. Yet most of these writers pressed their arguments for traditional norms and forms of family and sexuality on nonbiblical and nontheological grounds. They also were sometimes sharply critical of the Bible—denouncing Saint Paul's preferences for celibacy, the Mosaic provisions on unilateral male divorce, and the tales of polygamy, concubinage, and prostitution among the ancient biblical patriarchs and kings. Moreover, most of these writers jettisoned many other features of the Western tradition that, in their judgment, defied reason, fairness, and utility—including, notably, the establishment of Christianity by law and the political privileging of the church over other associations. Their arguments were not a rationalist apologia for traditional Christian family values or a naturalist smokescreen for personal religious beliefs. They defended traditional family and sexual norms not out of confessional faith but out of rational and empirical proof, not just because they uncritically believed in these norms but because they made good sense and they worked for the most part.

But Enlightenment liberals and their modern heirs also pushed modern churches and states alike to reform their traditional family teachings and laws, often with enduring salutary results that both church and state still enjoy today. For example, Saint Paul and John Chrysostom had already stipulated that husbands and wives are "equal in dignity" and in "conjugal rights."[145] But it took Enlightenment thinkers like Mary Wollstonecraft and Frances Hutcheson to push the Western legal tradition to remove the many legal layers of patriarchy and coverture that had long obscured these ideals, and move the laws toward fuller equality and rights protection of women in public and private life.[146] These legal reforms came only gradually in later generations, and full gender equality in church, state, and society remains an aspiration. But the overt sexual double standards of the past are happily waning in most parts of the West.

Moses and Jesus had already called the faithful to make careful provision and protection for children, and both apostolic church constitutions and medieval canon laws already set out an ample roll of children's rights.[147] But it was Enlightenment liberals who insisted that these legal rights protections be greatly expanded and extended to all children, regardless of their race,

145 See sources and discussion in ibid., 28–29.

146 Ibid., 156–63.

147 Ibid., 258–59 and Witte, *The Sins of the Fathers*, 11–48.

gender, religion, culture, or birth status, and vindicated and protected by family, church, and state alike.[148] Not all Christian writers today accept the idea of children's rights, and the United States has refused to ratify the UN Convention on the Rights of Child, in large measure because of opposition from some Christian quarters.[149] Even so, both churches and states in the West now make ample provision for all children in their local ministries and policies.

Echoing the Hebrew Bible, Christian writers from the start have stipulated that marriages involve the union of "two in one flesh."[150] And they have warned against the dangers of plural marriage, even for faithful biblical patriarchs like Abraham, Jacob, David, and Solomon.[151] But it was the Enlightenment liberals who argued most strongly and consistently that polygamy causes or correlates with too many harms, violates the natural rights of women, children, and men alike, jeopardizes the political economy, and hampers the production of good citizens and orderly government.[152] Not all churches and states today, especially in the Global South, accept this teaching. But the Western case against polygamy remains legally strong and popularly convincing today, although the rights of polygamists will likely soon be a new "frontier of family law."[153]

Christian writers have long said that the household labor of wives and mothers is of great value to church, state, and society, and that divorcees and widows accordingly should receive alimony and dower payments after a marriage has ended. But it was Enlightenment liberals like Adam Smith and Jeremy Bentham who argued that a wife must have equal marital property and contract rights, and that a woman's household labor needs to be better calculated and capitalized both during marriage and after it has ended.[154] It took two centuries more for these egalitarian economic arguments to take stronger legal root. But modern law-and-economics scholars and feminist scholars alike have pressed this argument effectively in recent decades, and much more egalitarian marital property laws and postmarital property distributions are now a commonplace in the West, even if full gender equality remains an aspiration.

148 Witte, *Church, State, and Family*, 256–60.

149 Ibid., 238–56.

150 Genesis 2:24, Matthew 19:6, 1 Corinthians 6:16.

151 See John Witte, Jr., *The Western Case for Monogamy over Polygamy* (Cambridge: Cambridge University Press, 2015), 34–92.

152 Ibid., 348–88; Witte, *Church, State, and Family*, 288–93.

153 Mark A. Goldfeder, *Legalizing Plural Marriage: The Next Frontier in Family Law* (Lebanon, NH: Brandeis University Press, 2017).

154 Witte, *Church, State, and Family*, 165–80.

Christianity, Liberalism, and Same-Sex Marriage

These stories of creative convergence, if not reconciliation, of traditional teachings and modern liberties about sex, marriage, and family life offer hope for the battles over same-sex marriage that have torn Western churches, states, and families apart over the past half century, and will likely do the same in the Global South over the next century. Since the 1960s, same-sex parties moved rapidly from social ostracism to "marital equality," as the movement came to be named. This was a well-orchestrated cultural movement that eventually brought seismic legal changes to America and many other Western lands. From Stonewall to *Obergefell*, from community halls to corporate boardrooms, from local marches to a brilliant social media campaign, this marital equality movement pressed the case in favor of marriage for a new segment of the population. The movement made basic appeals to justice, liberty, and equality. It presented compelling stories of mutual love, support, and flourishing of same-sex couples and their children. It introduced new ways to think about the nature of sex and sexuality. It sparked new interpretations of traditional texts. It created new liturgies and ceremonies for communal investment in marriage formation. It offered new adoptive homes for orphans and new intact homes for other children. It offered new domestic resources to other community members. Despite a fifteen-hundred-year criminal ban on same-sex activities, let alone marriage, this marital equality movement gradually convinced growing segments of the population, and growing numbers of Western legislatures and courts—now in thirty plus Western nations and counting—to widen their definition of the marital family to include same-sex couples.

The legal battles over same-sex marriage in the West are largely over, and opinion polls suggest that this issue will likely die out in another generation or two. Unlike elective abortion, which will likely remain controversial because of the loss of innocent life involved, same-sex marriage does not involve the same kind of harm. Yes, some view the institution of marriage itself as a casualty of the battles over same-sex marriage and see its legalization as the beginning of the end of the marital family. But similar arguments were made when societies came to accept marriages between parties of different classes, races, ages, and religions. In every instance, the institution of marriage remained resilient, even if it became more inclusive. Yes, some view religious freedom as a casualty in the battle over same-sex marriage, with some religious individuals and groups now forced to accept, service, license, or bless a state-sanctioned form of marriage that they find deeply sinful, on pain of state fines, penalties, or losses of jobs, licenses, tax exemptions, corporate status, and more. But religious voices were on both sides of the same-sex marriage debate, and religious freedom is simply too fundamental a principle of liberal democracy to remain permanently subordinate to claims of sexual liberty. As recent Supreme Court and European Court of Human Rights cases are now making clear, religious freedom and same-sex liberty need to find ways of living together in a democratic society committed to freedom for all.[155] And yes, some view the West's decision to legalize same-sex marriage as the first step on the slippery slope to the complete "democratization of desire."[156] Indeed, some liberals treat the movements of the past half century for civil rights, same-sex marriage, and "disestablished" sexual liberty as parts and products of the same broader liberation from the shackles of religion, tradition, and institutionalization.[157] But classical liberals like David Hume already warned that state laws that permitted the return to a "libertine" sexual state of nature or promoted the fall of the organized marital household would spell "the doom" of human liberty and orderly society.[158] Modern liberals, in turn, warn against an unregulated sexual market where, in Anita Bernstein's apt words, "wealth (in men) and reproductive-age youth (in women) are cold commodities … pursued and bought and sold and liquidated even more harshly" than they are under current laws, with devastating results for many men, women, and children especially.[159]

Leading American family policy experts Jonathan Rauch and David Blankenhorn—once, respectively, a champion and the other an opponent of same-sex marriage[160]—more constructively view the legalization of same-sex marriage as an ultimate win for the institution of marriage. They call on culture warriors on both sides of the same-sex marriage debate to end their legal wrangling and constitutional brinksmanship, and instead work together to "make marriage achievable for all who seek it" and attractive to those who

155 See Witte, *Church, State, and Family*, 300–35; John Witte, Jr., *The Blessings of Liberty: Religious Freedom and Human Rights in the Western Tradition* (Cambridge: Cambridge University Press, 2021), 238–39; and John Witte, Jr., Joel A. Nichols, and Richard W. Garnett, *Religion and the American Constitutional Experiment*, 5th ed. (Oxford: Oxford University Press, 2022), 188–201.

156 The subtitle of Brian McNair, *Striptease Culture: Sex, Media, and the Democratization of Desire* (London: Routledge, 2002).

157 See, for example Carlos A. Ball, ed., *After Marriage Equality: The Future of LGBTQ Rights* (New York: NYU Press, 2017).

158 David Hume, *Essays: Moral, Political, and Literary*, rev. ed., ed. Eugene F. Miller (Indianapolis, IN: Liberty Fund, 1987), 187–90.

159 Anita Bernstein, "For and Against Marriage: A Revision," *Michigan Law Review* 102 (2003): 129–212, at 176.

160 David Blankenhorn, *The Future of Marriage* (New York: Encounter Books, 2007); Jonathan Rauch, *Gay Marriage: Why It Is Good for Gays, Good for Straights, and Good for America* (New York: Henry Holt and Company, 2013).

have given up on it. Marriage, whether straight or gay, is still "fundamental" today, they argue. "Marriage creates family and strengthens social bonds. It's a wealth-producing institution. It's almost certainly society's most pro-child institution. Warts and all, it's today's best bet if you are seeking faithfulness and lasting love."[161]

Before the legalization of same-sex marriage, Rauch and Blankenhorn argue, resistance to the modern sexual revolution was viewed as not only prudish but also prejudiced. Ever since the Moynihan Report in 1965 warned of the grave social dangers of the breakdown of the "black family," pro-marriage and pro-family movements were regarded as racist. Ever since the first Defense of Marriage Acts went on the federal and state books in the 1990s, pro-marriage movements were regarded as homophobic. But now pro-marriage movements are breaking out on economic lines, with the better educated and better off practicing stable marriages and child rearing, and those with fewer means and less education forgoing marital family life altogether, even while producing many children. Given these realities, Rauch and Blankenhorn argue, "marriage as culture war in America can now be replaced by marriage as common cause and a common conversation." Blacks and whites, straights and gays, liberals and conservatives, churches and states can all work together to "identify, reduce, and where possible eliminate social, economic, and legal barriers to marriage." "Liberals fighting for social justice and economic opportunity are now called by the logic of their values to help extend the advantages of marriage to low- and middle-income couples who seek it for themselves, much as they fought to help gay Americans attain marriage. Conservatives fighting for social stability and stronger families can now, based on the logic of their deepest values, recognize gays and lesbians who seek the same family values." If both sides can be gracious and generous in victory and defeat in the battle over same-sex marriage, Rauch and Blankenhorn conclude, the nation can get on with the larger legal and cultural struggle to protect and promote marital family life and responsible sex and parenthood for all.[162]

Fully agreed. But this noble aspiration will work only if some of the more radical same-sex marriage advocates stop viewing religious liberty as the enemy. Sexual liberty and religious liberty are both fundamental rights today, but religious liberty is a far more ancient protection, and it is a cornerstone of ordered liberty on whose proper protection many other human rights

161 "Marriage Opportunity: The Moment for National Action," p. 2, http://americanvalues.org/catalog/pdfs/Marriage-Opportunity.pdf.

162 Ibid., passim.

ultimately depend.[163] That idea is very much up for grabs today.[164] In the full flush of new victory and in angry retribution for centuries of mistreatment by the church, some LGBTQ advocates and media are attacking religious institutions that remain opposed to them and individual religious individuals who won't support their claims. They are labeling, boycotting, and publicly shaming as "bigots" and "hate groups" any churches, charities, law firms, NGOs, hospitals, adoption agencies, humanitarian groups, businesses, states, or others who don't embrace the full range of same-sex or transgender rights. But it is too much to expect all folks to sympathize with such public bullying, even if many of these same folks now accept same-sex marriage and harbor no ill against their LGBTQ neighbors. Many of the changes and accommodations that sexual liberty advocates are seeking need time to soak into a culture and slowly be reconciled with other interests. With patience, at least some of these changes will come. But pushing a radical agenda too far too fast will ultimately jeopardize many of the cultural and constitutional gains made by the LGBTQ community in recent years. Indeed, polls show that the promised protection of religious liberty against sexual liberty was one of the most decisive factors that has caused a hard right turn in American politics in recent years, and the bitter political tribalism that has resulted. European polls also show that the hard right turn in many countries is similarly fueled by popular dismay and rejection of the more radical agenda of some far-left LGBTQ groups. And many other parts of the world, not least in the fifty-seven Muslim-majority nations and in many Christian majority nations in the Global South, too, are deeply troubled by what Western liberalism has so radically and rapidly wrought and will likely delay any reforms in protection of their own same-sex citizens.

In turn, Western churches and other religious organizations would do well to rein in their anathemas and actions against same-sex marriage in public life and instead focus on improving the culture of the marital family more broadly both within and without the church. They would do well to shift from the massive and costly antiabortion and anticontraception campaigns of the past half century into a far more constructive and comprehensive pro-family campaign that includes attention to the hard issues of sexual promiscuity, teenage pregnancy, women's health, nonmarital birth, broken families, and encourages responsible marital sex, proper family planning, adoption reform, children's poverty relief, health care, education, and job training that are all so desperately in need of attention and reform. They would do well to root out and drive out all clergy and other religious leaders who abuse their wives, children,

163 See John Witte, Jr. and M. Christian Green, eds., *Religion and Human Rights: An Introduction* (New York: Oxford University Press, 2012).

164 Paul Horwitz, "The *Hobby Lobby* Moment," *Harvard Law Review* 128 (2014): 154, 155.

students, clients, patients, or parishioners, as well as their accomplices after the fact among the higher clergy or other supervisors who cover up these grave offenses. They would do well to be known for the countless quiet forms and forums of family service offered in modern sanctuaries, charities, schools, hospices, orphanages, diaconal centers, emergency shelters, foodbanks, counseling centers, health and humanitarian missions and programs. They would do well to foster the rich integrative understanding of marital and family love and fidelity that is taught in the Bible and echoed in countless catechisms, canons, and confessional documents over the centuries and still today.

The reality in the West today is that too many modern churches have lost their traditional role as exemplars of sexual morality and faithful family life. Too many churches have lost their capacity to engage the hard legal, political, and social issues of our day with doctrinal rigor, moral clarity, and canonical authenticity. Too often of late, Christians and other religious believers have marched to the culture wars without ammunition—substituting nostalgia for engagement, acerbity for prophecy, platitudes for principled argument, bumper sticker issues for holistic reformations. In centuries past, Catholic, Protestant, and Orthodox churches alike produced massive codes of religious law and moral discipline that covered many areas of life, not least sex, marriage, and family life. They instituted sophisticated tribunals for the equitable enforcement of these religious laws. They produced exquisite works of theology and jurisprudence that worked out the precepts of proper domestic living in detail. Some of that sophisticated legal work still goes on among some religious communities today. A growing cadre of Christian jurists, theologians, and ethicists are reengaging the hard questions. But the legal structure and institutional sophistication of modern churches are a pale shadow of what went on before. And many of their family norms and habits are increasingly devolving into simple variations on the cultural and legal status quo. Modern churches must think more seriously about restoring and reforming their own faith-based family laws on the strength of biblical and traditional family teaching, instead of simply acquiescing in state laws and culture. They must think much more seriously about their roles as "prophets, priests, and kings" in a secular age.

Bibliography

Abbott, Walter M., and Joseph Gallagher, eds. and trans. *The Documents of Vatican II*. New York: Guild Press, 1966.

Alexander, Michelle. *The New Jim Crow: Mass Incarceration in the Age of Colorblindness*. New York: Free Press, 2012.

Baker, Maureen, and Vivienne Elizabeth. *Marriage in an Age of Cohabitation*. Oxford: Oxford University Press, 2014.

Ball, Carlos A., ed. *After Marriage Equality: The Future of LGBTQ Rights*. New York: NYU Press, 2017.

Becker, Gary S. *The Economic Approach to Human Behavior*. Chicago: The University of Chicago Press, 1991.

Becker, Gary S. *A Treatise on the Family*. Cambridge, MA: Harvard University Press, 1991.

Becker, Gary S., and Kevin M. Murphy. "The Family and the State." *Journal of Law and Economics* 31, no. 1 (1988): 1–18.

Bellah, Robert N. "Epilogue: It Takes a Society to Raise a Family." In Steven M. Tipton and John Witte, Jr., eds., *Family Transformed: Religion, Values, and Society in American Life*, 286–98. Washington, DC: Georgetown University Press, 2005.

Bellah, Robert N. "Marriage in the Matrix of Habit and History." In Steven M. Tipton and John Witte, Jr., eds. *Family Transformed: Religion, Values, and Society in American* Life, 21–33. Washington, DC: Georgetown University Press, 2005.

Bellah, Robert N., Ann Swidler, William Sullivan, Richard Madsen, and Steven Tipton. *The Good Society*. New York: Vintage Books, 1991.

Bernstein, Anita. "For and Against Marriage: A Revision," *Michigan Law Review* 102 (2003): 129–212.

Bernstein, Anita, ed. *Marriage Proposals: Questioning a Legal Status*. New York: NYU Press, 2006.

Bishop, Joel Prentiss. *Commentaries on the Law of Marriage and Divorce, and Evidence in Matrimonial Suits*. 2nd ed. Boston: Little, Brown & Co., 1856.

Blackstone, William. *Commentaries on the Law of England*. 4 vols. Oxford: Clarendon Press, 1765.

Blankenhorn, David. *The Future of Marriage*. New York: Encounter Books, 2007.

Blauwhoff, Richard J. "Tracing Down the Historical Development of the Legal Concept of the Right to Know One's Origins." In Katharina Boele-Woelki, ed. *Debates in Family Law Around the Globe at the Dawn of the 21st Century*, 145–70. Antwerp: Intersentia, 2009.

Boyd, Craig A. *A Shared Morality: A Narrative Defense of Natural Law Ethics*. Grand Rapids, MI: Brazos Press, 2007.

Brinig, Margaret F. *Family, Law, and Community: Supporting the Covenant*. Chicago: University of Chicago Press, 2012.

Brinig, Margaret F. *From Contract to Covenant: Beyond the Law and Economics of the Family*. Cambridge, MA: Harvard University Press, 2000.

Brinig, Margaret F., and Steven L. Nock. "Can Law Shape the Development of Unconditional Love in Children?" In Timothy P. Jackson, ed., *The Best Love of the Child: Being Loved and Taught to Love as the First Human Right*, 317–46. Grand Rapids, MI: Eerdmans, 2011.

Brinig, Margaret F., and Steven L. Nock. "'I Only Want Trust:' Norms and Autonomy." *Journal of Socio-Economics* 32 (2003): 471–87.

Brinig, Margaret F., and Steven L. Nock. "Legal Status and Effects on Children." *University of St. Thomas Law Journal* 5 (2008): 548–79.

Browning, Don S. "The Best Love of the Child? An Integrational View." In Timothy P. Jackson, ed., *The Best Love of the Child: Being Loved and Being Taught to Love as the First Human Right*, 365–71. Grand Rapids, MI: Eerdmans, 2011.

Browning, Don S. *Equality and the Family: A Fundamental Practical Theology of Children, Mothers, and Fathers in Modern Society*. Grand Rapids, MI: Eerdmans, 2007.

Browning, Don S. "Family Law and Christian Jurisprudence." In John Witte, Jr. and Frank S. Alexander, eds. *Christianity and Law: An* Introduction, 163–185. Cambridge: Cambridge University Press, 2008.

Browning, Don S. "Legal Parenthood, Natural and Legal Rights, and the Best Interests of the Child: An Integrative View." In Linda C. McClain and Daniel Cere, eds., *What Is Parenthood: Contemporary Debates about the Family*, 105–23. New York: NYU Press, 2013.

Browning, Don S. *Marriage and Modernization: How Globalization Threatens Marriage and What to Do about It*. Grand Rapids, MI: Eerdmans, 2003.

Browning, Don S. "A Natural Theory of Marriage." *Zygon*, 46 (2011): 733–60.

Browning, Don S. *Reviving Christian Humanism: The New Conversation on Spirituality, Theology, and Psychology*. Minneapolis, MN: Fortress Press, 2010.

Browning, Don S., et al. *From Culture Wars to Common Ground: Religion and the American Family Debate*. 2nd ed. Louisville, KY: Westminster John Knox Press, 2000.

Browning, Don S., and Gloria G. Rodriguez. *Reweaving the Social Tapestry: Toward a Public Philosophy and Policy for Families*. New York: W. W. Norton, 2002.

Browning, Don S., and John Witte, Jr. "Emil Brunner." In John Witte, Jr. and Gary S. Hauk, eds., *Christianity and Family Law: An Introduction*, 307–22. Cambridge: Cambridge University Press, 2017.

Browning, Don S., M. Christian Green, and John Witte, Jr., eds. *Sex, Marriage and Family in the World Religions*. New York: Columbia University Press, 2006.

Broyde, Michael J. *Sharia Tribunals, Rabbinical Courts, and Christian Panels: Religious Arbitration in America and the West*. Oxford: Oxford University Press, 2017.

Broyde, Michael J., and Michael Ausubel, eds. *Marriage, Sex, and Family in Judaism*. Lanham, MD: Rowman & Littlefield, 2005.

Brundage, James A. *Law, Sex, and Christian Society in Medieval Europe*. Chicago: University of Chicago Press, 1987.

Bunge, Marcia J., ed. *The Child in Christian Thought and Practice*. Grand Rapids, MI: Eerdmans, 2000.

Burnside, Jonathan P. *God, Justice, and Society: Aspects of Law and Legality in the Bible*. Oxford: Oxford University Press, 2011.

Cahill, Lisa Sowle. *Family: A Christian Social Perspective*. Minneapolis: Fortress Press, 2000.

Cahill, Lisa Sowle. *Sex, Gender and Christian Ethics*. Cambridge: Cambridge University Press, 1991.

Campbell, Carolyn. *Together Again: True Stories of Birth Parents and Adopted Children Reunited*. New York: Berkley Books, 1999.

Carbone, June, and Naomi Cahn. *Marriage Matters: How Inequality Is Remaking the American Family*. Oxford: Oxford University Press, 2014.

The Catechism of Modern Man. Boston: Daughters of St. Paul, 1968.

Cere, Daniel. "Canadian Conjugal Mosaic: From Multiculturalism to Multiconjugalism?" In Joel A. Nichols, ed., *Marriage and Divorce in a Multi-Cultural Context: Multi-Tiered Marriage and the Boundaries of Civil Law and Religion*, 284–308. Cambridge: Cambridge University Press, 2011.

Cere, Daniel. "Toward an Integrative Account of Parenthood." In Linda C. McClain and Daniel Cere, eds. *What Is Parenthood: Contemporary Debates about the Family*, 19–40. New York: NYU Press, 2013.

Chapais, Bernard. *Primeval Kinship: How Pair-Bonding Gave Birth to Human Society*. Cambridge, MA: Harvard University Press, 2008.

Code of Canon Law: Latin-English Translation. London: Collins, 1983.

Code of Canons of the Eastern Churches: New English Translation. Washington, DC: Canon Law Society of America, 1998.

Coons, John E. "The Religious Rights of Children." In John Witte, Jr. and Johan D. van der Vyver, eds. *Religious Human Rights in Global Perspective: Religious Perspectives*, 157–74. The Hague: Martinus Nijhoff Publishers, 1996.

Coons, John E., and Patrick M. Brennan. *By Nature Equal: The Anatomy of a Western Insight*. Princeton: Princeton University Press, 1999.

Descartes, René. *Discours de la Méthode* [1637]. Paris, Larousse, 1934.

De Waal, Frans B. M. *Our Inner Ape: A Leading Primatologist Explains Why We Are Who We Are*. New York: Riverhead Books, 2006.

De Waal, Frans B. M. *A Tree of Origin: What Primate Behavior Can Tell Us about Human Evolution*. Cambridge, MA: Harvard University Press, 2002.

The Digest of Justinian. Edited by Theodor Mommsen and Paul Krüger, translated by Alan Watson. 4 vols. Philadelphia: University of Pennsylvania Press, 1985.

Doe, Norman. *Christian Law: Contemporary Principles*. Cambridge: Cambridge University Press, 2013.

Doe, Norman, ed. *Christianity and Natural Law: An Introduction*. Cambridge: Cambridge University Press, 2017.

Domingo, Rafael. "Body, Soul, and Spirit of the Law: Toward a Holistic Legal Paradigm." *Oxford Journal of Law and Religion* 7 (2018): 230–49.

Domingo, Rafael, and Gonzalo Rodríguez-Fraile Díaz. *Spiritualizing Humanity*. N.p. 2022.

Douglas, Gillian. "Marriage, Cohabitation, and Parentage—From Contract to Status?" In Sanford N. Katz, John Eekelaar, and Mavis Maclean, eds. *Cross Currents. Family Law and Policy in the US and England*, 211–33. Oxford: Oxford University Press, 2000.

Epstein, Louis M. *Marriage Laws in the Bible and Talmud*. Cambridge, MA: Harvard University Press, 1942.

Elazar, Daniel J. *Covenant and Polity in Biblical Israel: Biblical Foundations and Jewish Expressions*. London: Transaction Publishers, 1998.

Ellickson, Robert. *The Household: Informal Order around the Hearth*. Princeton, NJ: Princeton University Press, 2008.

Erikson, Erik. "The Development of Ritualization." In Donald R. Cutler, ed., *The Religious Situation*, 711–33. Boston: Beacon Press, 1968.

Ettelbrick, Paula L. "Since When Is Marriage a Path to Liberation?" *Outlook: National Gay and Lesbian Quarterly* 6 (Fall 1989): 9–13.

Evans, Michelle, and Augusto Zimmermann, eds. *Global Perspectives on Subsidiarity*. Dordrecht: Springer, 2014.

Falk, Ze'ev W. *Jewish Matrimonial Law in the Middle Ages*. Oxford: Oxford University Press, 1966.

Farley, Margaret A. *Just Love: A Framework for Christian Sexual Ethics*. New York: Continuum, 2008.

Federal Interagency Forum on Child and Family Statistics. *America's Children: Key National Indicators of Well-Being*. Washington, DC: U.S. Government Printing Office, 2015.

The Federalist Papers: Alexander Hamilton, James Madison, and John Jay. Edited by Ian Shapiro. New Haven, CT: Yale University Press, 2009.

Fleming, James E., and Linda C. McClain. *Ordered Liberty: Rights, Responsibilities, and Virtues*. Cambridge, MA: Harvard University Press, 2013.

Finnis, John. *Human Rights and Common Good*. Oxford: Oxford University Press, 2011.

Fivush, Robyn. *Family Narratives and the Development of an Autobiographical Self*. London: Routledge, 2019.

Fivush, Robyn, and Judith A. Hudson, eds. *Knowing and Remembering in Young Children*. Cambridge: Cambridge University Press, 2013.

Flannery, Austin, ed. *Vatican Council II: Volume 2, More Postconciliar Documents*. New rev. ed. Dublin: New Dominican Publication, 1998.

Franklin, Robert M. *Crisis in the Village: Restoring Hope in African American Communities*. Minneapolis, MN: Fortress Press, 2007.

Franklin, Robert M. "Rehabilitating Democracy: Restoring Civil Rights and Leading the Next Human Rights Revolution." *Journal of Law and Religion* 30 (2015): 414–27.

Garrison, Marsha. "The Decline of Formal Marriage: Inevitable or Reversable?" *Family Law Quarterly* 41 (2007–08): 491–520.

Garrison, Marsha. "Marriage Matters: What's Wrong with the ALI's Domestic Partnership Proposal." In Robin Fretwell Wilson, ed., *Reconceiving the Family: Critique on the American Law Institute's Principles of the Law of Family Dissolution*, 305–30. New York: Cambridge University Press, 2006.

Garrison, Marsha. "Reviving Marriage: Could We? Should We?" *Journal of Law and Family Studies* 10 (2007–08): 279–335.

Garrison, Marsha. "Toward a Contractarian Account of Family Governance." *Utah Law Review* (1998): 241–69.

Garrison, Marsha, and Elizabeth Scott, eds. *Marriage at the Crossroads: Law, Policy, and the Brave New World of Twenty-First Century Families*. Cambridge: Cambridge University Press, 2013.

George, Robert P., and Gerard V. Bradley. "Pope John Paul II." In John Witte, Jr. and Gary S. Hauk, eds., *Christianity and Family Law*, 363–80. Cambridge: Cambridge University Press, 2017.

George, Robert P., and Jean Bethke Elshtain. *The Meaning of Marriage*. New York: Scepter Publishers, 2010.

Girgis, Sherif, Ryan T. Anderson, and Robert P. George. *What Is Marriage? Man and Woman: A Defense*. New York: Encounter Books, 2012.

Glendon, Mary Ann. *Abortion and Divorce in Western Law*. Cambridge, MA: Harvard University Press, 1987.

Goldfeder, Mark A. *Legalizing Plural Marriage: The Next Frontier in Family Law*. Lebanon, NH: Brandeis University Press, 2017.

Goodwin, Michele Bratcher, ed. *Baby Markets: Money and the New Politics of Creating Families*. Cambridge: Cambridge University Press, 2010.

Decretum Magistri Gratiani, ed. Emil Friedberg; repr. ed. Graz: Akademische Druck- u. Verlagsanstalt, 1959.

Gray, Peter B., and Kermyt G. Anderson. *Fatherhood: Evolution and Human Paternal Behavior*. Cambridge, MA: Harvard University Press, 2010.

Grubbs, Judith Evans et al., eds. *The Oxford Handbook of Childhood and Education in the Classical World*. Oxford: Oxford University Press, 2014.

Helfand, Michael A. "Arbitration's Counter-Narrative: The Religious Arbitration Paradigm." *Yale Law Journal* 124 (2015): 2994–3051.

Helmholz, R. H. *Natural Law in Court: A History of Legal Theory in Practice*. Cambridge, MA: Harvard University Press, 2015.

Henrich, Joseph, Robert Boyd, and Peter J. Richerson. "The Puzzle of Monogamous Marriage." *Philosophical Transactions of the Royal Society B*, 367 (2012): 657–69.

Hillers, Delbert R. *Covenant: The History of a Biblical Idea*. Baltimore, MD: Johns Hopkins University Press, 1969.

Hittinger, Russell. *The First Grace: Rediscovering the Natural Law in a Post-Christian World.* Wilmington, DE: ISI Press, 2014.

Hittinger, Russell. "Society, Subsidiarity, and Authority in Catholic Social Thought." In Patrick M. Brennan, ed. *Civilizing Authority: Society, State, and Church*, 119–44. Lanham, MD: Lexington Books, 2007.

Hobbes, Thomas. *Leviathan*. Edited by Noel Malcolm. Oxford: Oxford University Press, 2011.

Hogan, Richard M., and John M. Levoir. *Covenant of Love: Pope John Paul II on Sexuality, Marriage and Family in the Modern World.* Garden City, NY: Doubleday, 1985.

Horwitz, Paul. *First Amendment Institutions*. Cambridge, MA: Harvard University Press, 2013.

Horwitz, Paul. "The *Hobby Lobby* Moment." *Harvard Law Review* 128 (2014): 154–92.

Hugenberger, Gordon P. *Marriage as Covenant: A Study of Biblical Law and Ethics Governing Marriage Developed from the Perspective of Malachi.* Leiden: Brill, 1994.

Justinian's Institutes. Translated by Peter Birks and Grant McLeod. Ithaca, NY: Cornell University Press, 1987.

Kammen, Michael G. *Spheres of Liberty*. Jackson: University of Mississippi Press, 2011.

Kippley, John F. *Sex and the Marriage Covenant: A Basis for Morality*. Cincinnati, OH: CCL, 1991.

Konner, Melvin A. *The Evolution of Childhood: Relations, Emotions, Mind*. Cambridge, MA: Harvard University Press, 2010.

Landes, Elisabeth M., and Richard A. Posner. "The Economics of the Baby Shortage." *The Journal of Legal Studies* 7 (1978): 323–48.

Lawler, Michael G. "Marriage as Covenant in the Catholic Tradition." In John Witte, Jr. and Eliza Ellison, eds., *Covenant Marriage in Comparative Perspective*, 70–92. Grand Rapids, MI: Eerdmans, 2005.

Lazar, Harvey, and Christian Leuprecht, eds. *Spheres of Governance*. Montreal/Kingston: McGill-Queens University Press, 2007.

Locke, John. *Two Treatises of Government* [1689]. Edited by Peter Laslett. Cambridge: Cambridge University Press, 1960.

Long, Joseph R. *A Treatise on the Law of Domestic Relations*. 3rd ed. Indianapolis: Bobbs-Merrill, 1923.

Macedo, Stephen. *Just Married: Same-Sex Couples, Monogamy & the Future of Marriage.* Princeton, NJ: Princeton University Press, 2015.

Mackin, Theodore. *What Is Marriage?* New York: Paulist Press, 1982.

Marquardt, Elizabeth. *My Daddy's Name Is Donor: A New Study of Young Adults Conceived through Sperm Donation.* New York: National Marriage Project, 2011.

McAdams, Richard H. *The Expressive Powers of Law: Theories and Limits*. Cambridge, MA: Harvard University Press 2015.

McClain, Linda C. *The Place of Families: Fostering Capacity, Equality, and Responsibility*. Cambridge: Cambridge University Press, 2006.

McNair, Brian. *Striptease Culture: Sex, Media, and the Democratization of Desire*. London: Routledge, 2002.

Menander Rhetor. Translated and edited by D. A. Russell and N. G. Wilson. Oxford: Oxford University Press, 1981.

Moughtin-Mumby, Sharon. *Sexual and Marital Metaphors in Hosea, Jeremiah, Isaiah, and Ezekiel*. Oxford: Oxford University Press, 2008.

Montesquieu, Baron de. *The Spirit of the Laws* [1748]. Translated by Thomas Nugent. New York: Hafner Publishing Co. 1949.

Nelson, William T. *A Treatise on the Law of Divorce and Annulment of Marriage*. Chicago: Callaghan, 1895.

Novak, David. *Covenantal Rights: A Study in Jewish Political Theory*. Princeton, NJ: Princeton University Press, 2009.

Novak, David. *Natural Law in Judaism*. Cambridge: Cambridge University Press, 2008.

Novak, David. *The Jewish Social Contract: An Essay in Political Theology*. Princeton, NJ: Princeton University Press, 2009.

Nussbaum, Martha C. "A Right to Marry?" *California Law Review* 98 (2010): 667–96.

O'Donovan, Oliver. *Begotten or Made?* Oxford: Oxford University Press, 2002.

O'Donovan, Oliver. *Entering into Rest: Ethics as Theology*. Vol. 3. Grand Rapids, MI: Eerdmans, 2017.

O'Donovan, Oliver. *Resurrection and Moral Order: An Outline for Evangelical Ethics*. Grand Rapids, MI: Eerdmans, 1986.

Osiek, Carolyn, and David Balch. *Families in the New Testament World: Households and House Churches*. Louisville, KY: Westminster John Knox Press, 1997.

Orme, Nicholas. *Medieval Children*. New Haven, CT: Yale University Press, 2001.

Palmer, Paul F. "Christian Marriage: Contract or Covenant." *Theological Studies* 33 (1972): 617–65.

Pontifical Council for Justice and Peace. *Compendium of the Social Doctrine of the Catholic Church*. London: Burns and Oates, 2012.

Pope John Paul II. *Familiaris Consortio* (On the Role of the Christian Family in the Modern World), http://w2.vatican.va/content/john-paul-ii/en/apost_exhortations/documents/hf_jp-ii_exh_19811122_familiaris-consortio.html.

Payer, Pierre. *Sex and the Penitentials: The Development of a Sexual Code, 500–1550*. Toronto: University of Toronto Press, 1994.

Perdue, Leo G., ed. *The Family in Ancient Israel*. Louisville, KY: Westminster John Knox Press, 1997.

Plato. *Symposium*. Translated by Alexander Nehamas and Paul Woodruff. Indianapolis: Hackett Publishing Co., 1989.

Plato. *The Complete Works*. Translated and edited by Bernard Jowett. New York: Random House, 1965.

Pope, Stephen J. *Human Evolution and Christian Ethics*. Cambridge: Cambridge University Press, 2011.

Posner, Eric A. *Law and Social Norms*. Cambridge, MA: Harvard University Press, 2000.

Posner, Eric A. ed. *Social Norms, Nonlegal Sanctions and the Law*. Northampton, MA: Edward Elgar, 2007.

Posner, Richard A. *Sex and Reason*. Cambridge, MA: Harvard University Press, 1992.

Posner, Richard A. "The Regulation of the Market in Adoptions." *Boston University Law Review* 67 (1987): 59–72.

Post, Stephen B. *Spheres of Love: Toward a New Ethics of the Family*. Dallas, TX: Southern Methodist University Press, 1994.

Rauch, Jonathan. *Gay Marriage: Why It Is Good for Gays, Good for Straights, and Good for America*. New York: Henry Holt and Company, 2013.

Redmont, Esther. *The Economics of the Family*. 2 vols. Santa Barbara, CA: ABC-CLIO LLC, 2015.

Regan, Milton C., Jr. *Alone Together: Law and the Meanings of Marriage*. Oxford: Oxford University Press, 1999.

Regan, Milton C., Jr. "Calibrated Commitment: The Legal Treatment of Marriage and Cohabitation." *Notre Dame Law Review* 76 (2000–01): 1435–66.

Regan, Milton C., Jr. *Family Law and the Pursuit of Intimacy*. New York: NYU Press, 1993.

Reynolds, Philip L. *How Marriage Became One of the Sacraments*. Cambridge: Cambridge University Press, 2016.

Reynolds, Philip L., and John Witte, Jr., eds. *To Have and to Hold: Marrying and its Documentation in Western Christendom, 400–1600*. Cambridge: Cambridge University Press, 2007.

Rubio, Julie Hanlon. *A Christian Theology of Marriage and Family*. New York: Paulist Press, 2003.

Sacks, Jonathan. *The Home We Build Together: Recreating Society*. London: Continuum, 2007.

Sawhill, Isabel V. *Generation Unbound: Drifting into Sex and Parenthood without Marriage*. Washington, DC: Brookings Institution Press, 2014.

Searle, Mark, and Kenneth W. Stevenson, eds. *Documents of the Marriage Liturgy*. Collegeville, MN: Liturgical Press, 1992.

Schillebeeckx, Edward. *Marriage: Secular Reality and Saving Mystery*. London: Sheed and Ward, 1965.

Schneider, Carl E. "The Channeling Function in Family Law." *Hofstra Law Review* 20 (1992): 495–532.

Schneider, Carl E., and Margaret F. Brinig. *An Invitation to Family Law: Principles, Process, and Perspectives*. 3rd ed. St. Paul, MN: West Publishing, 2006.

Schneider, David M. *A Critique of the Study of Kinship*. Ann Arbor: University of Michigan Press, 1984.

Schroeder, H. J. *Councils and Decrees of the Council of Trent*. St. Louis: B. Herder Book Co., 1941.

Schouler, James, and Arthur W. Blakemore. *A Treatise on the Law of Marriage, Divorce, Separation, and Domestic Relations*. 6th ed. Albany, NY: M. Bender & Co., 1921.

Schulhofer, Steven J. *Unwanted Sex: The Culture of Intimidation and the Failure of Law*. Cambridge, MA: Harvard University Press, 2000.

Scott, Elizabeth S. "A World Without Marriage." *Family Law Quarterly* 41 (2007): 537–66.

Scott, Elizabeth S., and Robert E. Scott. "From Contract to Status: Collaboration and the Evolution of Novel Family Relationships." *Columbia Law Review* 115 (2015): 293–374.

Scott, Elizabeth S., and Robert E. Scott. "Marriage as Relational Contract." *Virginia Law Review* 84 (1998): 1225–334.

Song, Robert, and Brent Waters, eds. *The Authority of the Gospel: Explorations in Moral and Political Theology in Honor of Oliver O'Donovan*. Grand Rapids, MI: Eerdmans, 2015.

Stevenson, Kenneth W. *Nuptial Blessing*. New York: Oxford University Press, 1982.

Stone, Linda. "Kinship Back on Track: Primatology Unravels the Origin and Evolution of Human Kinship." *Evolutionary Psychology* 6, no. 4 (October 1, 2008).

Story, Joseph. *Commentaries on the Conflict of Laws, Foreign and Domestic, In Regard to Contracts, Rights, and Remedies, and Especially in Regard to Marriages, Divorces, Wills, Successions, and Judgments*. Boston: Hilliard Gray & Co., 1834.

Tach, Laura M., and Alicia Eads. "Trends in the Economic Consequences of Marital and Cohabitational Dissolution in the United States." *Demography* 52 (2015): 401–32.

Thaler, Richard H., and Cass R. Sunstein. *Nudge: Improving Decisions about Health, Wealth, and Happiness*. New York: Penguin Books, 2008.

Tipton, Steven M., and John Witte, Jr. *Family Transformed: Religion, Values, and Society in American Life*. Washington, DC: Georgetown University Press, 2005.

Van Drunen, David. *Divine Covenant and Moral Order: A Biblical Theology of Natural Law*. Grand Rapids, MI: Eerdmans, 2014.

Van Drunen, David. *Political Theology and Natural Law: Justice, Commerce, and Community Under Noah's Rainbow*. Grand Rapids MI: Zondervan Academic, 2020.

Waite, Linda J., and Maggie Gallagher. *The Case for Marriage: Why Married People Are Happier, Healthier and Better Off Financially*. New York: Broadway Books, 2001.

Wall, John, Don Browning, William J. Doherty, and Stephen Post, eds. *Marriage, Health and the Professions*. Grand Rapids, MI: Eerdmans, 2002.

Walzer, Michael. *Spheres of Justice: A Defense of Pluralism and Equality*. New York: Basic Books, 2010.

Wilson, Robert A. "The Primal Path to Kinship: A Critical Review of Bernard Chapais, Primeval Kinship: How Pair-Bonding Gave Birth to Human Society." *Biology & Philosophy* 25 (2010): 111–23.

Wilson, Robin Fretwell, ed. *Reconceiving the Family: Critique on the American Law Institute's Principles of the Law of Family Dissolution*. Cambridge: Cambridge University Press, 2006.

Witte, John, Jr. *The Blessings of Liberty: Human Rights and Religious Freedom in the Western Legal Tradition*. Cambridge: Cambridge University Press, 2021.

Witte, John, Jr. *Church, State, and Family: Reconciling Traditional Teachings and Modern Liberties*. Cambridge: Cambridge University Press, 2019.

Witte, John, Jr. "The Covenant of Marriage: Its Biblical Roots, Historical Influence, and Modern Uses." *INTAMS Review on Marriage and Spirituality* 18 (2012): 147–65.

Witte, John, Jr. *From Sacrament to Contract: Marriage, Religion, and Law in the Western Tradition*. 2nd ed. Louisville, KY: Westminster John Knox Press, 2012.

Witte, John, Jr. *The Sins of the Fathers: The Law and Theology of Illegitimacy Reconsidered*. Cambridge: Cambridge University Press, 2009.

Witte, John, Jr. *The Western Case for Monogamy over Polygamy*. Cambridge: Cambridge University Press, 2015.

Witte, John, Jr., and Eliza Ellison, eds. *Covenant Marriage in Comparative Perspective*. Grand Rapids, MI: Eerdmans, 2005.

Witte, John, Jr., and Gary S. Hauk, eds. *Christianity and Family Law: An Introduction*. Cambridge: Cambridge University Press, 2017.

Witte, John, Jr., Joel A. Nichols, and Richard W. Garnett. *Religion and the American Constitutional Experiment*. 5th ed. Oxford: Oxford University Press, 2022.

Witte, John, Jr., and M. Christian Green, eds. *Religion and Human Rights: An Introduction*. New York: Oxford University Press, 2012.

Witte, John, Jr., Michael Welker, and Stephen Pickard, eds. *The Impact of the Family on Character Formation, Ethical Education, and the Communication of Values in Late Modern Pluralistic Societies*. Leipzig: Evangelische Verlagsanstalt, 2022.

Wolfe, Christopher, ed. *The Family, Civil Society, and the State*. Lanham, MD: Rowman and Littlefield, 1998.

Yamin, Priscilla. *American Marriage: A Political Institution*. Philadelphia: University of Pennsylvania Press, 2012.

Ziettlow, Amy, and Naomi Cahn. "The Honor Commandment: Law, Religion, and the Challenge of Elder Care." *Journal of Law and Religion* 30 (2015): 229–59.

www.ingramcontent.com/pod-product-compliance
Lightning Source LLC
Chambersburg PA
CBHW031332230926
51848CB00001B/197
* 9 7 8 9 0 0 4 5 2 8 6 1 1 *